PM Teacher's Guide

Red / Yellow

Raewyn Hickey

Nelson
Nelson House
Mayfield Road
Walton-on-Thames
Surrey KT12 5PL
United Kingdom

Text © Raewyn Hickey, 2000
Published by Nelson, 2000
ISBN 0-17-402785-0
9 8 7 6 5 4 3 2 1
03 02 01 00

This teacher's guide contains references to the PM books written by Beverley Randell, Annette Smith, Jenny Giles and Mandi Rathbone.

We would also like to thank Nelson Thomson Learning Australia for permission to reprint the following poems:

Walking through the jungle	*My sore knee* by Beverley Randell
Monkey, Monkey	*In the gym* by Beverley Randell
Snuffle	*A shady hat* by Beverley Randell
Percy Pig	*Little grey kitten* by Zheyna Gay
The merry-go-round	*A spike of green* by Barbara Baker
The snowman's song by Beverley Randell	*My hippo* by Beverley Randell
Five little candles	*The pirate*
Spring	*Fish* by Arthur S Bourinot
The daisy	*My shell*
A ball by Jenny Giles	*A little birdsong*
Ten fat sausages	*Pets*
The owl	*Playing football* by Jenny Giles
Bumper cars by Beverley Randell	*The steam shovel* by Rowena Bennett
'So there', said Nick	*White rabbit*
This little teddy	*My helicopter*
My treasure by Jenny Giles	*Two Jurassic dinosaurs* by Beverley Randell
Lazy old lizard	

Please note. We have tried to trace and contact all copyright holders before publication, but this has not always been possible. If notified, we, the publishers will be pleased to make any amendments or arrangements at the first opportunity.

All rights reserved. No part of this publication may be reproduced, copied or transmitted in any form or by any means, electronic or mechanical, including photocopy, recording, or any information storage and retrieval system, without permission in writing from the publisher or under licence from The Copyright Licensing Agency Ltd., 90 Tottenham Court Road, London W1P 0LP.

Cover design and typeset by Jordan Publishing Design

Printed in Great Britain

The publisher grants permission for copies of pages 84–86 to be made without fee as follows:

Private purchasers may make copies for their own use or for use by their own students: school purchasers may make copies for use within and by the staff and students of the institution only.

This permission to copy does not extend to additional institutions or branches of an institution, which should purchase a separate master copy of the book for their own use.

For copying in other circumstances, prior permission must be obtained in writing from Nelson.

Contents

Introduction

Features of the PM programme	4–5
About PM	6
The importance of taking reading records	9
Reading record proforma example	11
Guided reading	13
Supported reading	17
What makes effective literacy teachers?	18
Red/Yellow components chart	20–21
PM Library families chart	22
List of Red/Yellow titles	23

Books at Red level

The photo book	24
Hedgehog is hungry	25
Wake up, Dad	36
Tiger, Tiger	27
The lazy pig	28
The merry-go-round	29
The little snowman	30
A birthday cake for Ben	31
Baby Lamb's first drink	32
Sally and the daisy	33
The big kick	34
Sausages	35
Pussy and the birds	36
The baby owls	37
The bumper cars	38
The flower girl	39
Ben's Teddy Bear	40
Ben's treasure hunt	41
Lizard loses his tail	42
Father Bear goes fishing	43
Tom is brave	44
Hide and seek	45
A home for Little Teddy	46
Where is Hannah?	47
Eggs for Breakfast	48
Red and Blue and Yellow	49
Look Up, Look Down	50
A Roof and a Door	51
Tall Things	52
Two Eyes, Two Ears	53

Books at Yellow level

Where are the sunhats?	54
Blackberries	55
Brave Father Mouse	56
Mumps	57
The hungry kitten	58
Sally's beans	59
Baby Hippo	60
Jolly Roger, the pirate	61
Lucky goes to dog school	62
Ben's dad	63
The new baby	64
Baby Bear goes fishing	65
Hermit Crab	66
Sally and the sparrows	67
Choosing a puppy	68
Football at the park	69
Seagull is clever	70
Little Bulldozer	71
Sally's red bucket	72
A friend for little white rabbit	73
Fire! Fire!	74
A Lucky Day for Little Dinosaur	75
Tiny and the big wave	76
Snowy gets a wash	77
My Dad	78
Our Mum	79
My Little Sister	80
My Big Brother	81
Our Baby	82
My Gran and Grandad	83

Assessment material

Assessment checklist	84
Reading record proformas	
Where is Hannah?	85
Snowy gets a wash	86
Work planning guides and NCS correlations	87

Introduction

Features of the PM programme

What distinguishes PM from other reading schemes? On these pages we have highlighted some of the features unique to PM:

The PM programme is divided into a number of **mini-series, which feature the same characters**. These books are carefully designed to look similar, enabling children to make meaningful comparisons between covers, layout, illustrations and design.

All the stories feature **well shaped plots**, which hold children's interest until the end of the story. Each is characterised by a problem or tension early on, which is satisfactorily resolved. **A range of narrative devices** is carefully introduced, preventing so-called 'scheme blindness' which can result from an unvaried programme of similar text types.

◀ **Characters' behaviour and personality in the recurring titles remain constant**, allowing pupils to build up character profiles. Sally, a nature-loving child who lives alone with her mum, demonstrates her resourcefulness in several titles. Note how **the language mimics natural speech** patterns and rhythms, making the story easy to read. Repetition of high-frequency words, plus **a controlled introduction rate of one new word in every 20** allows children to read with confidence.

The characters featured in the stories (whether human, animal or animation) **are portrayed as successful problem-solvers** and are treated with respect. However, these stories do not shirk issues of exclusion or rejection, allowing the teacher to raise them within the security of a fictional context with a positive resolution.

◀ The inclusion of narrative non-fiction books at each level allows pupils to become familiar with the conventions of different text types, which are nonetheless very accessible to emergent readers.

Included in the Storybooks is a ▶ range of science titles containing accurate information combined with careful and detailed illustrations presented in an accessible narrative format.

In addition to the points highlighted above, the PM titles avoid any form of stereotyping, racism or sexism, implicit or explicit. So Tom helps his Grandad cook supper, Ben cannot sleep without his teddy bear, Hannah climbs to the very top of the ladder in the gym and Matt is allowed to cry when his dog, Tiny, disappears under a wave. There is a range of genres and settings from the everyday to fantasy and cartoon. This is reflected in the illustrative styles used.

About PM

Introduction

> In the early stages, pupils should have a carefully balanced programme of guided reading from books of graded difficulty…These guided reading books should have a cumulative vocabulary, sensible grammatical structure and a lively and interesting content.
> *The National Literacy Strategy Framework for Teaching (1998)*

> Effective teachers of literacy 'believed that the creation of meaning in literacy was fundamental…(and) prioritised the creation of meaning in their literacy teaching…'
> *Effective Teachers of Literacy (May 1998)*

One of the key skills in the National Curriculum for teaching reading is
'…contextual understanding, focusing on meaning derived from the text as a whole'.

A powerful criticism levelled at many graded reading books, written for beginner readers, is that most are not stories, but repetitious reading exercises with little or no plot.

Books that will hold a young reader's interest have:
- tension;
- a climax;
- a satisfying ending.

Many teachers turned away from skills-based, over-repetitive, non-literary texts in favour of library picture books with literary merit, only to find that too many children are overwhelmed when confronted with the amount of new learning presented on each page.[1]

The PM Storybooks combine the virtues of both approaches by their:
- story structure;
- meaning;
- grading;
- matching of illustrations and text.

The quality of the stories is assured because every story adheres to the traditional story structure:
- tension (caused by a problem);
- climax (the 'will he/won't he?' moment);
- resolution (the problem is solved) with a positive ending that is an emotional necessity for young readers.

What makes PM an ideal programme for guided reading?

1. Reading is enjoyable

The use of the traditional story structure ensures that:
- children are motivated to read on to find out what happens next;
- there is a satisfying ending;
- there are opportunities for the development of logical thought and the understanding of cause and effect.

2. Meaning is paramount

One of the cues most often used by teachers to help children self-correct is the question: 'Does that make sense?'.

---

[1] A distinction must be made between 'new learning' and the amount of text on the page. When deciding upon the readability of a text, it can be misleading to assume that few words indicate an easy text. Conversely, it is often assumed that a higher number of running words indicates a difficult text. Teachers can rest assured that the PM Storybooks, with their relatively high number of running words, are nevertheless entirely suitable for their pupils.

The belief in the importance of self-correction has shaped every story. The PM Storybooks:
- are written about concepts that children can grasp – the reader is never bewildered;
- have the minimum of surprise twists in the plots so that children can use their developing skills of prediction and reasoning.

The books are carefully structured to give teachers opportunities to teach children how to use phonic cues and how to combine them with other sorts of information. Exemplary phonics instruction builds on a child's rich concept about how the printed word functions and is integrated into a total reading programme.

3. Correct level of difficulty

Careful grading ensures that children avoid frustrated attempts at reading:
- one new word is introduced in every twenty;
- each book draws on the same growing collection of high-frequency words;
- clear sentence structures are used consistently;
- language is related to children's experience of stories and spoken English;
- sentence construction becomes more complex as the children's skills develop;
- most books contain specialised interest words allowing for variety in subject matter.

4. Picture cues

The illustrations in every book are meticulously drawn to help children gain maximum understanding as they match picture and text. In the PM Storybooks, the illustrations are an integral part of the story and push the meaning along.

What makes PM an ideal programme for independent reading?

Children learn to read by reading. Because of the careful grading of the PM Storybooks, if children can read one, they should be able to read the next and the next. Steady success produces positive attitudes and leads to frequent and voluntary re-reading for pleasure; which leads to the consolidation of reading skills. There is no expectation of pre-teaching and practice before children can begin reading. The PM series ensures that words are meant to be deciphered in the books, in context, allowing for more practice and consolidation of reading strategies. This, in turn, leads to more independence, more skill with word analysis and greater joy.

Matching child to text

Reading means making sense of the print on the page. Skilled readers not only use the information contained in the print but also add to that information their knowledge of language and of the world. Skilled reading, therefore, is not a straightforward process of identifying all the letters and linking them into words which in turn become sentences. A skilled reader is concerned first with meaning and uses this to determine how much attention needs to be given to the print. Skilled readers have developed positive attitudes to reading, insisting that what they read makes sense and seeing books as relevant to their everyday lives.

It makes sense, then, to have children behaving as much as possible like skilled readers from the very beginning. It is the teacher's role to help children develop the strategies, understandings and attitudes that will give them a flexible self-improving system within which to develop their reading ability.

Sensitive observation of what a child is doing while reading provides the teacher with information about what reading behaviours the child has under his/her control, and what needs to be learned.

Emergent reading behaviours

1. Behaviours indicating knowledge of the way books work (concepts about print):
   - understands that the print conveys a message;
   - knows where to start reading;
   - knows the front and back of a book;
   - can indicate the title;
   - understands the left page is read before the right;
   - understands the concept of a word/letter;
   - can identify the top and bottom of a page;
   - can match word by word while reading a line of print;
   - can return to the left and continue reading if there is more than one line of print.

2. Behaviours indicating early strategies:
   - predicts what makes sense;
   - uses information from pictures;
   - uses knowledge of oral language to predict;
   - uses initial letters to make predictions;
   - can locate familiar words;
   - notices similarities and differences in words.

3. Behaviours indicating independence:
   - self-monitors using word-by-word matching;
   - uses knowledge of familiar words to notice a mis-match;
   - remembers language patterns;
   - actively works to solve mis-matches before requesting help;
   - can sustain reading behaviour alone.

Selecting appropriate texts

In addition to observing a child's behaviour whilst reading, a careful evaluation of the text *per se* as well as a consideration of the child's history are important when matching child to text. For instance, if you are using a selection of reading resources outside the PM series, you may wish to consider the following:
- What background experience is required of the reader?
- How relevant are the theme and topic?
- Is the content accessible?
- If the book contains facts, are these so diluted that the reader will have to unlearn them at a later stage?
- Is the form appropriate for the content?
- Is the length appropriate?
- Do the language and style suit the topic?
- Does the direct speech sound natural or contrived?
- What connectives are used, and how?
- Is the typeface suitable in terms of size, style and spacing?
- Do the illustrations complement or overwhelm the text?

While all these factors have been very carefully considered in creating the PM series, there are nonetheless situations where an individual child's experience may deviate from the norm. For instance, *Ben's dad* tells the story of Ben's excitement at his dad's return home. (His dad is a sailor who spends a considerable amount of time at sea.) A child who has a violent parent may associate the return of this parent with dread, rather than excitement. This is not to say that this child cannot read or enjoy *Ben's dad*; however, the teacher will need to supply additional support in giving the child the text to read.

Children are capable of enjoying and appreciating texts which span a range of challenges, provided the text is accompanied by the appropriate level of support.

If the book offers only one or two challenges, and the child is able to read 95–100% of the words with confidence, then the text is suitable for independent reading.

If there are some new challenges and the child can read approximately 90% of the words with confidence, then the text is probably suitable for guided reading.

If the number of challenges is more or less equal to the number of familiar features, the text is probably suited to shared reading.

Children can also enjoy challenging and demanding texts which are read to them by the teacher.

The diagram below shows the relationship between level of support and type of text.

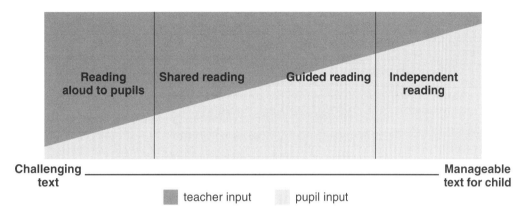

The importance of taking reading records

The effective teachers (of literacy) had very clear assessment procedures, usually involving a great deal of focused observation and systematic record-keeping. This contributed markedly to their abilities to select appropriate literacy content for their children's needs.

Effective Teachers of Literacy, page 44 (May 1998)

Monitoring is at the heart of the reading programme, and central to effective monitoring is the technique of taking reading records. Reading records describe accurately the child's reading and are a tool for scoring and analysing precise reading behaviours. They enable teachers to:
- find the appropriate instructional level for the child;
- group children for guided reading;
- know what the child can currently do;
- know what reading strategies a child is using;
- determine the next step for instruction;
- move children from one level of book to another.

Taking a reading record involves no more preparation than sitting beside a child with pencil and paper while he/she reads a text. The teacher does not need a separate copy of the text. Usually the text will be one that the child has read once or twice before and that the teacher has predicted will offer a small degree of challenge. The text should not be so difficult that the child's ability to process the information will break down.

The teacher's role

- Code everything the child reads on a form or blank sheet of paper.
- Do not teach.
- When a child needs help, wait, then give him/her the word.

All reading behaviour is recorded on a reading record, including both errors and self-corrections. The teacher counts the number of errors to calculate the child's instructional level.

When a child is reading at his/her instructional reading level, the text will have a degree of challenge suitable for his/her developing reading strategies while providing enough material for the child to read without error so that the reading process does not break down. Marie Clay suggests that when the accuracy percentage is between 90% and 94% the child is reading at the correct instructional level. If the error rate is up to one in 20 words (5%) the text is easy and may be read independently. A text which the child reads with an error rate of more that one in 10 words (10%) is hard and the child will struggle to maintain any reading strategies.

What counts as an error?

- no response (and the teacher has told the child the word);
- miscues (if the same word is read inaccurately more than once it is counted as an error each time although errors with proper nouns are counted only once);
- omissions (if a line is missed out, each word is counted as an error);
- insertions.

Useful conventions for taking reading records

- Mark every work read correctly by the student with a tick:

    ✓ ✓ ✓ ✓
    The hippos are asleep.

- Record all attempts and errors by showing the student's responses above the text:

    sit
    He is safe

- If the student self-corrects an error, record it as a self-correction, not an error:

    come | sc
    Here they | come

- If a word is left out or there is not response, record it as a dash and call it an error:

    —
    in the river, too.

- If a word is inserted, record it and call it an error:

    the
    Can you see ∧ Baby Hippo?

- If the student is told by the teacher, record it with a 'T' and call it an error:

    Baby Hippo is safe | T

- If the student appeals for a word, say 'You try it'. If unable to continue, record 'A' for appeal, tell the student the word and call it an error:

    sit | see | A |
    safe | | | T

- Repetition is not counted as an error, but is shown by an 'R' above the word that is repeated, as well as the number of repetitions, if more than one:

    R   R³
    ✓   or   ✓

- Record 'R' for repeats plus an arrow if the student goes back over several words or even back to the beginning of the page:

    ←――――――――
    ✓ ✓ R✓
    The hippos are asleep,

- If the student appears confused, help by saying 'Try that again'. This is counted as one error only before that piece of text is reread:

    [Have the call]
    [Here they come.] TTA

What does not count as an error?

- self-corrections;
- repetitions.

These behaviours should be encouraged with specific praise such as 'I like the way you …'.

Teachers will want to analyse the reading record in terms of what the child finds difficult and if the child is using any strategies such as re-reading or looking at parts of words without prompting. Some errors would cause more concern than others. For instance the substitution of a word which does not make sense would give more concern than substituting 'the' for 'a'.

Error rate is calculated by counting the number of (running) words (RW) in the text and dividing that number by the number of errors (E).

For example: $\frac{RW}{E} = \frac{70}{5} = 1:14$

Below is a simple table for quickly converting the error rate into a percentage.

	Error rate	Percentage accuracy
Easy	1 : 100 1 : 50 1 : 35 1 : 25 1 : 20	99% 98% 97% 96% 95%
Instructional	1 : 17 1 : 14 1 : 12.5 1 : 11.75 1 : 10	94% 93% 92% 91% 90%
Hard	1 : 9 1 : 8 1 : 7 1 : 6 1 : 5	89% 87.5% 85.5% 83% 80%

An example of a reading record is shown on page 12. The text is taken from *Baby Hippo*, Yellow Level Set 1. Reading record proformas for *Where is Hannah?*, Red Level Set 3, and *Snowy gets a wash*, Yellow Level Set 3, are included on pages 85 and 86.

---

* **E** = Errors

S. C. = Self-correcting

MSV = Meaning
Structure of the sentence
Sources of visual information

Reading record

Name: Megan
Text: Baby Hippo
Age: 5.4
Level: Yellow Set 1
Accuracy: 93%
Date: 3/3/00
R. W.: 118
S. C. Rate: 1:5

Page		E*	S. C.*	Errors MSV*	Self corrections MSV*
1	The hippos are asleep, down↑ in the river. Can you see Baby Hippo?	1		M S V	
2	Baby Hippo is in the river, too. He is asleep on Mother Hippo's back. He is safe. (sit)	1 1		Ⓜ Ⓢ V M S Ⓥ	
6	The lions are asleep in the sun. They like the sun. (The|SC)	1		Ⓜ Ⓢ Ⓥ	Ⓜ Ⓢ Ⓥ
8	The sun is going down.↑	1		M S V	
9	Mother Hippo is asleep, and Baby Hippo is going for a walk.				
10	The lions wake up. (woke) They are hungry.	1		Ⓜ Ⓢ Ⓥ	
11	Baby Hippo is not looking at the lions.				
12	The lions can see Baby Hippo. Here they come. (come|SC)	1		Ⓜ Ⓢ Ⓥ	Ⓜ Ⓢ Ⓥ
13	Mother Hippo wakes up. (woke) She sees the lions. (see)	1 1		Ⓜ Ⓢ Ⓥ Ⓜ S Ⓥ	
14	Here comes Mother Hippo! Mother Hippo is big. She is **too** big! The lions run away.				
15	The hippos are back in the river, and Baby Hippo is safe.↑	1			
* These abbreviations are explained on page 11. **TOTAL**		8	2	M S V 6 5 5	M S V 2 2 2

Example of an Assessment Record © Nelson, 2000

Guided reading

> The effective teachers were able to identify their teaching purpose for children reading a text clearly and also to identify what they wanted children to learn from reading that text.
>
> *Effective Teachers of Literacy, page 35 (May 1998)*

The first stages of language growth are rooted in babies' efforts to grasp and convey meanings. A baby learning to talk will begin by using single words and the parent will respond as the context dictates. Often the parent will fill out the words for him/her. The child says 'Gone' and the mother responds with 'Yes, pussy has gone out the door'. Babies embark on the formidable task of learning to talk with the vigour characteristic of natural learners. Children learning to talk are adventurous in their use of language and are happy to take risks as a way of learning.

Children take risks when they are self-confident, and children who are learning to read must be as self-confident as they are when they are talking. They need to be able to copy adult reading behaviour in an environment that encourages, guides and supports without censure. A balanced literacy programme provides many opportunities for children to behave as listeners, readers, writers and literary critics.

The classroom should provide opportunities for children to:
- listen and respond to high-quality literature, both fiction and non-fiction;
- have access to computers, reference books and word processors;
- write their own texts;
- read and respond to their own and others' writing;
- see their own writing displayed and shared;
- be actively engaged in reading and writing.

There is plenty of evidence to show that children learn to read by reading. Expert readers are those who have developed a large repertoire of skills through practice in purposeful reading. Practice should not be in the form of repetitive exercises or drills but should mirror the way in which a child learns to talk or walk or ride a bike; practice in reading should be with texts where children feel confident in taking risks and consolidating previous learning.

A balanced reading programme provides opportunities for children to respond to texts in various ways.

In shared reading, the text should be rich and challenging and beyond the current ability of the majority of the class. The teacher provides a high level of support, reading along with the children, modelling the behaviour of expert readers. The teacher leads the sessions from pre-planned objectives, teaching the children how print works on a page, making mistakes and modelling how to correct them, modelling risk-taking and setting up situations for children to predict the outcomes.

In guided reading, the teacher creates a situation where children can practise their current level of skill on a text which they can readily comprehend. The teacher carefully scaffolds the task so that the children can read at least 90% of the text and is on hand to guide the children into using their maturing skills to read those parts that are difficult.

Children must also be given the opportunity to practise their reading skills independently. For independent reading, the texts can be drawn from a variety of sources:
- shared reading texts;
- library books;
- familiar guided-reading texts;
- games;
- instructions;
- other children's published writing;
- displays around the room.

There is little or no support. The reader independently solves problems while engaging in reading for meaning.

> Guided reading is at the heart of a balanced literacy programme. Guided reading is the vehicle by which children can move from understanding about print and book language to being able to access the printed word independently.
> - It provides opportunities for risk-taking within a supportive environment;
> - It provides opportunities for children to develop their reading strategies;
> - It is carefully scaffolded so that the children are never put in a position of failure;
> - It gives children enjoyable experiences of reading for meaning;
> - It builds in the steps for children to become independent readers.

Independence in reading is not achieved by learning letter-sound relationships. It is a much larger cognitive enterprise relating to thinking and understanding, and governed by feedback and self-correction processes.

Marie Clay in *Becoming Literate: The Construction of Inner Control*
Heinemann page 254, (1991)

The structure of a guided reading lesson

	Purpose	**Teacher**	**Child**
Book introduction	• to explain the plot, story line, how this text works; • to introduce character names; • to clarify a concept; • to introduce new vocabulary.	• goes through the text discussing the illustrations; • asks questions to focus the children's attention on the story line; • asks questions to focus children's attention on new vocabulary and sentence structures.	• responds to the teacher's questions; • predicts from the illustrations.
Reading the text	• children practise their reading strategies; • children attempt new strategies with teacher support.	• listens in to monitor and to work with individual children; • assists through questioning; • develops children's reading strategies.	• reads the whole text quietly; • attempts self-correction strategies; • practises new strategies.
Responding to the text	• teacher pre-plans a teaching point.	• focuses children's attention on a feature of the text at word, sentence or text level.	• responds to the text as a reader; • relates the text to own experience; • learns a spelling pattern or new word.

An example of the interactions between a teacher and a child reading a guided reading text

Tiger, Tiger **by Beverley Randell, PM Storybook Red Level Set 1**
Child and teacher read the title together.
Child reads title page.

Page 3
Child: *Tiger is ...*   (Text: Tiger is asleep.)
Teacher: *Look at the picture. What is Tiger doing?*
Child: *Sleeping.*
Teacher: *Read it again and get your mouth ready to say the last word.*
Child: *Tiger is a ... Tiger is asleep.*

Page 5
Child: *Baby Monkey is asleep.*   (Text: Mother Monkey is asleep.)
       Mother Monkey is asleep.   (Text: Baby Monkey is asleep.)
Teacher: *That was very good reading but which one comes first, Mother Monkey or Baby Monkey? Read it again and look carefully at the beginning of the words.*
Child: *Mother Monkey is asleep.*
Teacher: *How did you know that was 'Mother Monkey'?*
Child: *There is an 'M'.*
Teacher: *And what would 'Baby' start with?*
Child: *'B'.*
Teacher: *Well done. I liked the way you noticed that.*

Page 6
Child: *Baby Monkey ...*   (Text: Baby Monkey wakes up.)
Teacher: *Baby Monkey was asleep. Look at him now.*
Child: *Baby Monkey ...*
Teacher: *I liked the way you went back to the beginning to try again. Say the sound.*
Child: *'W'.*
Teacher: *Look at the Baby Monkey and then read it again.*
Child: *Baby Monkey w ...wakes up.*

Prompts (cues) to support the use of strategies

During guided reading, the goal for the teacher is to assist the children to use effective strategies for working on text, not to accumulate items of knowledge. Children will develop self-correction strategies through effective questioning by the teacher.

> The range of strategies can be depicted as a series of searchlights, each of which sheds light on the text. Successful readers use as many of these strategies as possible.
>
> *The National Literacy Framework, DfEE, 1998*

As teachers, our aim is to teach children that there is more than one way of tackling a difficulty. Different kinds of information can be checked against each other to confirm a response. Children need to notice an error themselves and correct it independently. This is called self-monitoring.

Questions to develop reading behaviour

The strategy the child needs to develop determines the type of question the teacher asks.

Self-monitoring

To encourage and foster self-monitoring, look for opportunities when the child hesitates:

Say: I liked the way you stopped. What did you notice?
I liked the way you tried to work that out.
What do you expect to see at the beginning/end/after that?
Try again from the beginning of the sentence.

Meaning

Help the child to predict from the picture/context. Encourage the child to take risks.

Say: Look at the picture.
You said…Does that make sense?
What do you think will happen next?

Grammatical knowledge

Help the child to use words correctly.

Say: You said 'I haved a toy'. Can we say it that way?
It's the same on every page. Read the previous page again.

Visual awareness

Help the child to look carefully at the words and their parts.

Say: Does it look like…?
Does it look right?
What does it start with?
Yes, it could be … but look at the end.

Encouraging self-correction

Allow time for the child to notice an error for himself/herself:

Say: You made a mistake on that page/in that sentence. Can you find it?

Classroom management

> Key factors in successful implementation (of the National Literacy Hour) include good classroom management technique and sound classroom routines that promote independent working. Underpinning all of this is an emphasis on the effective management of children's behaviour and teachers' expectations of high standards of discipline and challenging learning activities.
>
> *The National Literacy Strategy,* Module 1

During the Literacy Hour, the teacher of an infant class is expected to teach two guided reading groups. Following a guided reading session the teacher is likely to set an activity for the group directly related to the guided reading text which may be completed that day or the following day. The rest of the class need to be able to work independently at a range of literacy activities which could include:

- re-reading familiar guided reading books;
- re-reading the big books;
- reading known poetry/nursery rhymes/jingles/songs;
- reading library books in the book corner;
- reading each other's published stories;
- listening to tapes;
- computer games and stories;
- alphabet games;
- matching texts and pictures;
- writing.

Supported reading

In many classrooms, teachers have additional support from classroom assistants. Classroom assistants can work with children in various ways during the independent session of the Literacy Hour by:
- hearing individual children read;
- playing a game;
- supervising a task;
- supporting children as they revisit a guided reading text.

Supported reading of a guided reading text is similar to hearing individual children read, and follows the same structure as a guided reading session:
- discussing the illustrations in the book;
- clarifying concepts;
- children reading the text;
- revisiting the text.

The children will have read the story during a guided reading session with the teacher, so the initial run-through of the text looks at:
- retelling the story;
- supporting the retelling by finding evidence in the text;
- relating the story to the children's own experiences where possible;
- reinforcing concepts, for example: what 'waves' are, what we mean by 'seasons'.

As the children read the text quietly to themselves, the classroom assistant listens to a little bit of reading from each child, praising when the child attempts self-correction and helping the child at a difficult word.

Specific praise encourages the child to attempt the same strategies again when a problem is encountered. Say, for example:
- I liked the way you went back to the beginning of the sentence/line to try that again.
  (The child has noticed an error and is attempting to correct it.)
- I liked the way you made that make sense.
  (The child has attempted the word.)

Use prompts that will help children solve a problem.
- Say, 'Look at the picture and think about…'
- Ask a question related to the meaning, for example: 'What was he doing?'
  'What do you think he would say?'
- Repeat what the child has said and ask 'Does that sound right?'
  (The child has used the wrong grammatical structure, such as: 'come' instead of 'came'.)
- Ask, 'What sound does it make at the beginning? What word would make sense and start that way. Read it again.'
  (The child has made no attempt at the word.)

After the reading, ask questions to which children can respond personally:
- 'Which part of the story made you feel sorry for…/did you find funny/made you realise what would happen next?'
- 'Why did you like this story?'
- 'What other stories have you read about these characters/made you feel the same way/had the same theme?'
- 'What experiences have you had at the seaside/with a pet that made you feel angry/sad/happy?'

What makes effective literacy teachers?

A report commissioned by the Teacher Training Agency into understanding more clearly how effective teachers help children to become literate drew the following conclusions.

Effective teachers:
- believed that the creation of meaning in literacy was fundamental;
- involved the children in problem-solving for themselves rather than giving the children 'facts' to learn;
- used teaching activities 'which explicitly emphasised the deriving and creating' of meaning;
- made the purpose of the reading and writing tasks clear to children;
- embedded word and sentence level aspects of reading and writing in whole-text activities which were explained clearly to pupils. Teachers in the validation sample were more likely to teach isolated skills which the children did not necessarily relate to the wider purpose of using those skills in reading and writing;
- taught such skills as phonics, spelling, grammar etc. ensuring that children had a clear understanding as to their importance and function;
- conducted their lessons at a brisk pace, providing time frames to keep children on task;
- used the classroom environment to display examples of print and regularly drew the children's attention to what was on the walls;
- had very clear assessment procedures involving observations and systematic record keeping;
- selected appropriate tasks to suit their children's needs;
- had a clear system of organisation;
- used the diagnostic information they had gathered on children to inform their planning and teaching.

Importance of assessment and planning

> Our best policy is to monitor actual behaviour as the child carries out the task in a meaningful situation – such as normal reading and writing within the programme – and to compare such observations with those taken for the same child at some previous time.
>
> Don Holdaway in *The Foundations of Literacy*, page 168 (Ashton Scholastic 1979)

A clear picture of what a child can *currently* do informs the teacher what needs to be learned next. A teacher is concerned to find out each child's:
- reading strategies;
- understandings about reading;
- developing attitudes to reading.

As part of base-line assessment when a child first enters school, the teacher will need to find out if each child:
- speaks English as a first or second language and, if English is a second language, the degree of fluency;
- is confident in talking to teachers and peers;
- is able to respond to questions;
- is able to carry out directions;
- shows an interest in books;
- listens to stories with interest;
- returns to known stories, poems and songs;
- uses the illustrations to retell stories;
- can read competently already;
- realises that print conveys a message.

Early assessments are regularly amended so that the individual child is catered for within a group. The class programme should fit the child, and not vice versa. Some children will move more slowly through the stages of development. Most of these children do not require a different approach, but more opportunity for reading practice.

Teachers will need to take regular running records in order to assess accurately an individual child's progress and development of reading strategies. (See **'The importance of taking running records'** on page 9).

Assessment

Assessment often results in immediate adjustments being made to group composition and the choice of reading texts.

Assessment should include:
- observation of a child's interaction with books;
- monitoring of the high-frequency words a child knows;
- monitoring of the letters a child knows;
- running records.

This type of diagnostic assessment should directly influence the teacher's planning.

Planning

- Initially teachers should test children for the number of letters and/or words they know. This will be a rough guide when beginning to group children for instruction;
- Teachers need to choose books from the Magenta Level according to which high-frequency words need to be reinforced and which new word needs to be taught;
- Children need to be able to recognise about 15 high-frequency words before moving onto the Red level even if they get over 94% accuracy in a running record;
- Children will probably have between 25 and 30 high-frequency words before moving to the Yellow level, although teachers will need to make accurate assessments with running records.

COMPONENTS

MAGENTA LEVEL

Working towards Level 1 →

Alphabet Starters	Alphabet Blends	Readalongs	Starters One	Starters Two
26 fiction titles	34 fiction titles	18 titles with audio cassettes	20 titles	20 titles

RED LEVEL

Working towards Level 1 →   Working within Level 1

Red Set 1	Red Set 2	Red Set 3	Non-fiction Maths around us
8 fiction titles	8 fiction titles	8 fiction titles	6 titles

YELLOW LEVEL

Working within Level 1 →

Yellow Set 1	Yellow Set 2	Yellow Set 3	Non-fiction Families around us
8 fiction titles	8 fiction titles	8 titles	6 titles

BLUE LEVEL

Working within Level 1 →

Blue Set 1	Blue Set 2	Blue Set 3	Non-fiction People around us
8 fiction titles	8 fiction titles	8 fiction titles	6 titles

GREEN LEVEL

Working within Level 1 →   Working towards Level 2

Green Set 1	Green Set 2	Green Set 3	Non-fiction Time and seasons
8 fiction titles	8 fiction titles	8 fiction titles	6 titles

ORANGE LEVEL

Working towards Level 2 →

Set A	Set B	Set C	Traditional Tales and Plays	Non-fiction Pets
6 fiction titles	6 fiction titles	6 fiction titles	6 titles	6 titles

TURQUOISE LEVEL

Working towards Level 2 →   Working within Level 2

Set A	Set B	Set C	Traditional Tales and Plays	Non-fiction Animal in the wild
6 fiction titles	6 fiction titles	6 fiction titles	6 titles	6 titles

PURPLE LEVEL

Working within Level 2 →

Set A	Set B	Set C	Traditional Tales and Plays	Non-fiction Farm animals
6 fiction titles	6 fiction titles	6 fiction titles	6 titles	6 titles

GOLD LEVEL

Working within Level 2 →   Working towards Level 3

Set A	Set B	Set C	Traditional Tales and Plays	Non-fiction Nocturnal animals
6 fiction titles	6 titles	6 fiction titles	6 titles	6 titles

SILVER LEVEL

Working towards Level 3 →   Working within Level 3

Set A	Set B	Set C	Traditional Tales and Plays	Non-fiction Polar animals
6 fiction titles	6 fiction titles	6 fiction titles	6 titles	6 titles

EMERALD LEVEL

Working within Level 3 →

Set A	Set B	Set C	Anthology
6 fiction titles	6 fiction titles	non-fiction titles	64 pages

CHART

RED LEVEL

PM Story Books

Reading Recovery Levels

PM Non-fiction – Maths around us

YELLOW LEVEL

PM Story Books

PM Non-fiction – Families around us

This chart provides an overview of where and how Red and Yellow Levels fit into the PM scheme. The daisy logo on the back cover of each individual title provides an at-a-glance guide to the book's difficulty: the colour of the solid petal corresponds to the colour level to which that book belongs. Three petals are allocated to each colour band; the position of the solid petal indicates the level of difficulty within that colour band. Non-fiction titles span the upper end of one colour band and the lower level of the next. They act as bridging texts from one level to the next.

Red and Yellow Level are emergent texts. Children reading Red Level Storybooks in guided reading are working towards Level 1 of the National Curriculum.

Children reading Red Level non-fiction and Yellow Level texts in guided reading are working within Level 1.

Red Level is suitable for most children in Y1 terms 1–2.

Yellow Level is suitable for most children in Y1 terms 2–3.

PM Library families chart

Protagonist(s)	Family description	Book title	Level
Sally	Sally and Mum are a single-parent family. Sally visits her Dad on Saturdays.	Sally's new shoes Sally and the daisy Sally's beans Sally and the sparrows Sally's red bucket Sally's friends Locked Out The island picnic	Magenta Starters Two Red Set 2 Yellow Set 1 Yellow Set 2 Yellow Set 3 Blue Set 1 Blue Set 3 Green Set 3
Ben	Nuclear family: Ben, Mum and Dad. Dad works at sea and so does not appear in many stories. Mum's love of books is apparent in the stories, and she also appears to be studying in some stories.	Ben's red car A birthday cake for Ben Ben's Teddy Bear Ben's treasure hunt Ben's dad The best cake Candle-light Ben's tooth	Magenta Starters Two Red Set 1 Red Set 3 Red Set 3 Yellow Set 2 Blue Set 2 Green Set 1 Green Set 2
Matt	Nuclear family: Matt, Mum and Dad, and their dog Tony.	My little dog Tiny and the big wave	Magenta Starters Two Yellow Set 3
James, Kate and Nick	Nuclear family: James, Kate, Nick, Mum and Dad. Nick/Nicola is a tomboy with a mind of her own. Her independent streak features in *The merry-go-round* and *The flower girl*.	The photo book Wake up, Dad The merry-go-round The bumper cars The flower girl Hide and seek Where are the sunhats? Snowy gets a wash	Red Set 1 Red Set 1 Red Set 1 Red Set 2 Red Set 2 Red Set 3 Yellow Set 1 Yellow Set 3
Rachel and Sam	Nuclear family: Rachel, Sam, Mum and Dad.	The little snowman Choosing a puppy Teasing Dad The flood After the flood The Biggest Fish	Red Set 1 Yellow Set 2 Blue Set 3 Green Set 3 Green Set 3 Orange Set A
Tom	Nuclear family: Tom, Mum and Dad. Baby Emma appears from *The new baby* onwards. Nana and Poppa are also introduced.	The big kick Sausages Tom is brave Mumps The new baby Birthday balloons The babysitter	Red Set 2 Red Set 2 Red Set 3 Yellow Set 1 Yellow Set 2 Blue Set 2 Green Set 2
Bears	Nuclear family: Father Bear, Mother Bear and Baby Bear.	Father Bear goes fishing Blackberries Baby Bear goes fishing Honey for Baby Bear Baby Bear's present Mushrooms for dinner House-hunting Father Bear's surprise	Red Set 3 Yellow Set 1 Yellow Set 2 Blue Set 1 Blue Set 1 Blue Set 3 Green Set 1 Green Set 2
Hannah	Hannah and Mum are the only characters we meet in these stories, and so we could assume that this is a single-parent family.	Where is Hannah? Try again, Hannah	Red Set 3 Green Set 3
Tim	We do not meet Tim's immediate family (except Mum), as most of these stories are set at the park or in the playground. *Late for football* is set at Tim's home. Tim's best friend Michael also features in the stories.	Football at the park Tim's favourite toy Come on, Tim Late for football The country race	Yellow Set 2 Blue Set 2 Blue Set 3 Blue Set 3 Green Set 3
Little Dinosaur	Follows Little Dinosaur's adventures, and his relationships with other animals and dinosaurs (especially Big Dinosaur, a predator).	A lucky day for Little Dinosaur The Dinosaur Chase Little Dinosaur Escapes A Troop of Little Dinosaurs	Yellow Set 3 Orange Set A Turquoise Set B Purple Set B

List of Red/Yellow titles

Red Level

Set 1
The photo book
Hedgehog is hungry
Wake up, Dad
Tiger, Tiger
The lazy pig
The merry-go-round
The little snowman
A birthday cake for Ben

Set 2
Baby Lamb's first drink
Sally and the daisy
The big kick
Sausages
Pussy and the birds
The baby owls
The bumper cars
The flower girl

Set 3
Ben's Teddy Bear
Ben's treasure hunt
Lizard loses his tail
Father Bear goes fishing
Tom is brave
Hide and seek
A home for Little Teddy
Where is Hannah?

Non-fiction – Maths around us
Eggs for Breakfast
Red and Blue and Yellow
Look Up, Look Down
A Roof and a Door
Tall Things
Two Eyes, Two Ears

Yellow Level

Set 1
Where are the sunhats?
Blackberries
Brave Father Mouse
Mumps
The hungry kitten
Sally's beans
Baby Hippo
Jolly Roger, the pirate

Set 2
Lucky goes to dog school
Ben's dad
The new baby
Baby Bear goes fishing
Hermit Crab
Sally and the sparrows
Choosing a puppy
Football at the park

Set 3
Seagull is clever
Little Bulldozer
Sally's red bucket
A friend for little white rabbit
Fire! Fire!
A lucky day for Little Dinosaur
Tiny and the big wave
Snowy gets a wash

Non-fiction – Families around us
My Dad
Our Mum
My Little Sister
My Big Brother
Our Baby
My Gran and Grandad

The photo book

Story by Beverley Randell
Illustrations by Elspeth Lacey

Level: Red Set 1
Genre: Story with predictable structure
Running words: 48
Links to other PM titles: *Wake up, Dad; The merry-go-round; The bumper cars; The flower girl; Hide and seek; Where are the sunhats?*

Overview

This story introduces James, Kate, Nick and their parents through the pictures in their family photo album. (In fact, this is a book within a book!) As we page through the album, we realise that one photo is missing. Whose can it be? The missing photo is of Teddy, and is supplied by Kate. Note the abbreviation of 'Nicola' to 'Nick', and what it might say about this character. You may wish to use this text to talk about families. How do we know the people in the photos belong to the same family?

Introducing the text

- Discuss the cover; relate to the children's own experiences of having a photograph taken; introduce the names of the children in the book.
- Discuss briefly all the pictures in the book. Draw the children's attention to the missing picture of Teddy on page 3 and ask them to speculate why there is no picture.
- Why is it important not to be left out? Should pets be included in the family album? Discuss the importance of inclusion.
- The illustration on page 15 should confirm predictions from previous discussion.

Reading the text

Children should read the whole text individually while the teacher reinforces known reading strategies and encourages those not yet mastered.

- Encourage children to read without finger pointing.
- Praise any self-correction, using phrases like 'I liked the way you noticed ...'
- Encourage children to re-read the preceding words when they get stuck.
- Encourage children who have finished first to re-read to themselves or a partner.

Revisiting the text

- Use magnetic letters to make 'Here'. Replace capital 'H' with lower case 'h' and ensure that the children recognise both words as being the same.
- Repeat the exercise, using other known words such as 'Look', 'Is' and 'It'.
- Make letter strings using 'book' such as 'look', 'took', 'cook'.
- Make sure the children have recognised 'too' as sounding the same as 'to'.

Writing activities

- Ask the children to bring photos of themselves or to draw themselves, or make a class/group photograph book.
- Ask the children to write a short biography under their picture.
- Ask them to make their own family photo book, illustrating each member of their family.
- Using phrases from the text, ask the children to write a sentence under each 'photo'.

Poems, rhymes and jingles

Here is a class song. Allow children to take turns to sing the questions and respond:

> Where is Lisa?
> Where is Lisa?
> Here I am
> Here I am
> I'm beside Simon
> I'm beside Simon
> Look at me
> Look at me.

Word level work	Sentence level work	Text level work	High-frequency words
To sight-read familiar high-frequency words and children's names.	To recognise the convention of using a capital letter to indicate names.	To understand words such as 'cover', 'author', 'title'.	here, is the, Mum, Dad, in, too

Hedgehog is hungry

Story by Beverley Randell
Illustrations by Drew Aitken

Level: Red Set 1
Genre: Story with predictable structure
Running words: 47
Links to other PM titles: *Can you see the eggs?* (Thematic); *Tiger, Tiger* (Thematic)

Overview
At the beginning of the story, it is winter and Hedgehog is asleep under a pile of leaves. The season changes to spring and Hedgehog wakes up. He is very hungry and goes looking for as many grubs as he can find to eat. Link this story to a science topic on the seasons or on mini-beasts, or use it as an opportunity to focus on the phoneme 'h'.

Introducing the text
- Discuss the first two pages using the vocabulary in the story (winter, hedgehog asleep), such as 'How can we tell it is winter?', 'Can you find Hedgehog?', 'What is he doing?'.
- On page 7 discuss what Hedgehog does in the spring.
- Encourage the children to predict what Hedgehog might eat and confirm this using the pictures.
- Use the last page to confirm how Hedgehog felt in the spring when he woke up.

Reading the text
- Children should read the whole text individually while the teacher reinforces known reading strategies and encourages those not yet mastered.
- Encourage children to read without finger pointing.
- Praise any self-correction using phrases such as, 'I liked the way you noticed ...'
- Teach the children to check their reading using two cues: meaning (picture) and visual (initial letter) cues, such as w- worm, c- caterpillar. Use phrases like, 'How did you know that was caterpillar?' (Because it starts with 'c'.)
- Encourage children who have finished first to re-read to themselves or to a partner.

Revisiting the text
- Discuss the use of alliteration in the title. Use the children's names or names of other animals to write other alliterative phrases, such as mouse is munching, worm is wiggling.
- Find other words that start with the same initial phoneme, such as 'Hedgehog' and 'hungry'.
- Discuss and list children's food preferences when they are hungry.
- Turn the list into a menu and put it on the wall or into a book for the children to re-read.

Writing activities
- Ask the children to make a group book of their food preferences.
- Make a wall chart or mobile of children's food preferences, such as 'Sasha likes baked beans'.
- Make an interactive display. Get the children to make a mural of the hedgehog and the things that he eats.
- Make labels that the children attach to the mural, such as 'Here is a snail'.

Guided writing activities
- Tell the children to re-read the text and discuss what grubs the hedgehog was thinking about when he woke up.
- Ask them to write the names in a list like a shopping list.
- Ask them to write a shopping list of the food they would like to eat if they could buy it for themselves. The children could then independently write lists for themselves.

Poems, rhymes and jingles

Little hedgehog
A hungry little hedgehog
Comes snuffling late at night
But when I go to see him
He rolls himself up tight
He turns into a prickly ball
With head and feet inside
This clever little hedgehog
Has the perfect way to hide.

Jenny Giles

Word level work	Sentence level work	Text level work	High-frequency words
To recognise phoneme/grapheme correspondence 'Hh'.	To expect the story to make sense and to use picture cues for meaning.	To track the text in the right order, page by page and from left to right.	is, here, up, a, the

Wake up, Dad

Story by Beverley Randell
Illustrations by Elspeth Lacey

Level: Red Set 1
Genre: Story with predictable structure
Running words: 67
Links to other PM titles: *The photo book; The merry-go-round; The bumper cars; The flower girl; Hide and seek; Where are the sunhats?*

Overview

This is a story about the family introduced in *The photo book*. In this story, Mum and the children have woken up before Dad. Each child in turn tries to wake Dad up but he keeps telling them that he is asleep. Finally, Mum joins in and they manage to push Dad out of bed and wake him up. The book can be linked to the theme of Myself and My Family.

Introducing the text

- Read the title and relate to the children's own experiences of waking up, or waking somebody else.
- Discuss what they would say.
- Discuss briefly all the pages in the book, introducing the language structures and words that the children and Dad said.
- Ask the children to predict whether Dad will wake up.
- Draw children's attention to the bold print on page 14.
- Draw children's attention to the change in the language pattern at the end.

Reading the text

- Children read the whole text individually.
- Encourage children to use cross-checking strategies, i.e. meaning cues (picture cues) with visual cues (initial letters) to read the children's names (K = Kate, J = James).
- Encourage children to read with pace and expression, making it 'sound like talking'.
- Encourage children to read without finger pointing.

Revisiting the text

- Discuss reasons why they might have wanted Dad to wake up.
- Write in an extra sentence, such as 'Wake up Dad, you promised to take us to the park'.
- Make a word string from 'wake' such as 'cake', 'lake', 'make', using magnetic letters.
- Ask the children to recognise and write the high-frequency words several times (up, look, is, am, Dad, Mum, at).

Writing activities

- Use two or three pages from the book and add speech bubbles. The children write in what each family member said, or might have said.
- Use the picture on page 3 and describe what is happening.
- Each child makes his or her own little book using text such as 'I am asleep', 'I am up'.

Guided writing activities

- Ask the children to re-read the text. Draw up a writing frame about their family members and what time they get up, such as 'My Dad ... (gets up first)', 'My Mum ...', 'My brother ...', 'My sister ...'

Other text level work

- Use the following poem with the class.

   Ten in the bed
   There were ten in the bed
   And the little one said
   'Roll over, roll over.'
   So they all rolled over
   And one fell out.

   There were nine in the bed
   And the little one said
   'Roll over, roll over.'
   So they all rolled over
   And one fell out.
   There was one in the bed
   And the little one said
   'GOODNIGHT!!'

Word level work	Sentence level work	Text level work	High-frequency words
To recognise high-frequency words used in text.	To use grammar to predict words.	To encourage children to be aware of story structure and how, in this story, structure is linked to Dad's refusal to get up.	Mum, Dad, is, in, up, look, am, at

Tiger, Tiger

Story by Beverley Randell
Illustrations by John Boucher

Level: Red Set 1
Genre: Story with predictable structure
Running words: 55
Links to other PM titles: *Hedgehog is hungry; Pussy and the birds; The baby owls* (Thematic)

Overview
Tiger wakes up and goes hunting for food. Will he eat Baby Monkey who has left the safety of his mother in the tree? Fortunately Mother Monkey wakes up just in time to save Baby Monkey. Ensure that your pupils understand the drama in this story, and that they make the connection between Tiger going hunting, and Baby Monkey sitting on the ground eating berries.
Tiger Tiger reinforces the words introduced in *Wake Up, Dad* and *Hedgehog is hungry*, as well as introducing some new vocabulary. The story is sequential and can be linked to time.

Introducing the text
- Read the title and discuss the initial letter sound of 'Tiger'.
- Ask the children to predict what the tiger would like to eat.
- Discuss the first four pages of the book using the language structure of the story, and asking the children what time of the day it is.
- Predict why Baby Monkey wakes up and what he is going to do.
- On pages 13 and 15 predict how the story will end. Will Baby Monkey be safe?

Reading the text
- Notice if the children have remembered the vocabulary from *Hedgehog is Hungry* or *Wake up, Dad*.
- Check that the children have noticed the 's' in 'comes' on page 15.
- Encourage the children to use visual cues (initial letters) to check whether the character is Baby Monkey or Mother Monkey.
- Encourage the children who have finished first to re-read to themselves or a partner.

Revisiting the text
- Discuss the characters and how they are feeling at certain points in the story.
- Make a chart of the different food that tigers and monkeys eat.
- Use magnetic letters to make 'wake' and 'come'; add 's' and point out how we have to read them now.
- Ask the children to see if they can write the known high-frequency words in a given time limit: is, up, the, here.
- Notice how 'Tiger' is written on pages 3 and 15. Why is it written with a capital letter at the end of a sentence? Look also at 'Baby Monkey' and 'Mother Monkey' to see if those words are written the same way.

Guided writing activities
- Use the structure of the story to write a sequel where the tiger wakes up and sees a different animal.
- Read the poem *Walking through the jungle* to the children and continue to innovate on the pattern:
  Walking through the jungle
  What did I see?
  A little baby monkey
  Laughing at me.

Poems, rhymes and jingles
Read the following poems to the class and add to the poetry box.

Walking through the jungle
Walking through the jungle
What did I see?
A little baby monkey
Laughing at me.
Walking through the jungle
What did I see?
A great big tiger
Snarling at me.

Monkey, monkey
Monkey, monkey up a tree
I see you and you see me.
Hang by your fingers
Hang by your toes,
But don't fall down
On your little brown nose.

Word level work	Sentence level work	Text level work	High-frequency words
To recognise initial phoneme/grapheme correspondence in 'Tiger', 'Baby', and 'Monkey'	To encourage children to check text to ensure that what has been read makes sense.	To re-read and recite poem *Walking through the Jungle* to experiment with similar rhyming patterns.	is, up, comes, here, in, the, tree

The lazy pig

Story by Beverley Randell
Illustrations by Trish Hill

Level: Red Set 1
Genre: Story with predictable patterns
Running words: 68
Links to other PM titles: *Baby Lamb's first drink* (Thematic)

Overview

It is morning in the farmyard, and all the farm animals are waking up. All, that is, except the pig, who carries on sleeping. The readers wonder whether he will get up too. The story is resolved as we see pig lumbering towards his food bowl. Lazy pig is also a greedy pig! This session could be used to introduce the long 'oo' sound to your children.

Introducing the text

- Discuss the concept 'lazy' within the context of this story.
- Discuss the concept 'sunrise' and what it would mean to the animals.
- Use page 12 to predict whether the lazy pig will get up.
- Ensure the children hear the word 'Cock-a-doodle-doo' when introducing the book. Ask the children to find the word on the page.

Reading the text

- Observe which children have mastered the high-frequency words.
- If children have difficulty beginning the reading, ask them to notice the initial letter and get ready to make that sound.
- Observe whether the children have noticed the change in the pattern of the story on page 11.
- If children read 'woman' on page 13, refer them to the initial letter cue and ask them to reread.

Revisiting the text

- Discuss reasons why the pig might not want to get up.
- Discuss reasons why the cow, the sheep and the rooster all woke up.
- Use 'moo' and 'doo' to introduce the long 'oo' sound, and link it to 'too' which was introduced in *The photo book*.
- Use pencil and paper or little white boards (laminated card) for children to write as many high-frequency words as they can within a time limit.

Writing activities

- Get the children to make a zig-zag book of other farm animals saying 'I am up.'.
- In a shared writing exercise, list sounds made by farm animals.
- In a shared writing exercise, write recounts of children's experiences of visits to a farm.
- Write a repetitive factual book about a farm after the style of 'Old MacDonald' such as:
  > On a farm there is a horse.
  > On a farm there is a pig.
- Focus on one animal and write a factual text, such as:
  > Horses eat grass.
  > They can run and gallop.
  > They can jump.
- Make a wall story, using each animal in the text and writing in speech bubbles.

Poems, rhymes, jingles

Snuffle
Snuffle is a friendly pig
With a very sniffy snout
He sniffle, sniffle, snuffles
Whenever he goes out.

Percy Pig
This is Percy Pig
He is very big
His little tail is curly
Very whirly twirly.

Word level work	Sentence level work	Text level work	High-frequency words
To recognise the long 'oo' sound.	To read animal sounds with appropriate expression.	To link personal experience to events in the story.	up, the, is, I, am, said, here, come

The merry-go-round

Story by Beverley Randell
Illustrations by Elspeth Lacey

Level: Red Set 1
Genre: Story with familiar settings
Running words: 82
Links to other PM titles: *The photo book; Wake up, Dad; The bumper cars; The flower girl; Hide and seek; Where are the sunhats?*

Overview
Set in the familiar context of a merry-go-round ride, this story explores the importance of personal choice and individuality. James and Kate are already on the merry-go-round, but Nick rejects all the rides that Dad points out. Will Nick miss out? At last Dad and Nick spot the horse, and the story concludes happily with all three children on the merry-go-round.

Introducing the text
- Discuss children's experiences on a merry-go-round.
- Remind the children about the names of the characters they met in *The photo book* and *Wake up, Dad*.
- Briefly explore why Nick is looking unhappy on page 9.
- Predict which ride Nick will choose.

Reading the text
- Use the speech in the text to encourage the children to read as though they're talking.
- If children confuse the names in the book, direct them to the initial letter cue and also notice the final letter. (James finishes with an 's'.)
- Check whether the children are using picture cues to confirm the animal names.
- Check whether the children are noticing the bold print for reading with expression.

Revisiting the text
- Discuss any experiences the children may have had which are similar to Nick's, when they have said 'No'.
- Discuss why Nick might have chosen the horse.
- Use magnetic letters to make 'Here', 'Look', 'Come'. Change the initial letter to lower case. Ask children to write the words in both upper and lower case. Ask them to find an example in the text where 'here' is used with an upper case letter and a lower case one.
- Make letter strings from 'pig' (big, dig, fig), or 'plane'. Draw children's attention to the fact that we have to replace both the 'p' and the 'l' to make new words.

Writing activities
- Using the names of the children in the group, write a wall story about them, using the equipment in a playground or the PE equipment. For example:
  Come here, Kazia. Here is a ball.
  Come here, Sasha. Here is a hoop.
- Use the names of the children in the group and put them in the story, for example:
  Kazia is up on a horse.
  Sasha is up on a pig.
- In a shared writing exercise, write a recount of the children's experiences at a fair or fun park.
- Sort the different merry-go-round rides into categories. What is similar about the rides that the children choose?

Poem, rhymes and jingles

The merry-go-round
The merry-go-round
Sings doodle-dee-dee
Oh, won't you come
And play with me?

Merry-go-round
Merrily round and round he goes
My roundabout horse has a silver nose
Silver saddle and silver rein
Merrily round we go again.

Word level work	Sentence level work	Text level work	High-frequency words
To develop sight reading skills of children's names.	To read with appropriate expression.	To apply word level skills through Guided Reading.	come, here, said, Dad, is, a, look, at, up, on, no

The little snowman

Story by Jenny Giles
Illustrations by Isabel Lowe

Level: Red Set 1
Genre: Story with familiar settings
Running words: 59
Links to other PM titles: *Choosing a puppy*

Overview

Rachel, Sam and their mum decide to make a snowman and, in doing so, show what can be achieved when everyone works together. Emphasise how everyone adds something to the snowman, including Dad, who adds the finishing touch when he arrives home from work.

Introducing the text

- Read the title, and relate to the children's own experience of snow and building snowmen.
- Although the characters' names are not given, make sure the children realise that one of them is speaking on pages 2, 4, 7, 8, 10, 11 and 14.
- The speaker changes to Mum on page 6 and page 12, and to Dad on page 16.

Reading the text

- Encourage the children to read 'like talking' by noticing the speech marks.
- Use the letters 'b' and 'm' to help children self-correct if there is a confusion between 'snowman' and 'snowball'.
- Encourage cross-checking between the picture cues and the initial letters to read 'eyes', 'mouth', 'nose', and 'scarf'.
- Use visual cues to discriminate between 'big' on page 4 and 'little' on page 6.

Revisiting the text

- Discuss what the children used to make the features on their snowman, and decide what else they could have used.
- Look at the illustration of Dad on page 14, and decide what job he does. Encourage the children to elaborate on the reasons for their answers.

- Give each child the letters to make 'look'. Ask them to scramble it up and make it again several times.
- Ask the children to write 'look' from memory.
- Segment and blend 'big'. Write it on the board as the children say the letters.

Writing activities

- Make a potato man with the group and write captions:
  'Here is the … .'
  or
  'Look at the … .'
- Draw a large snowman for the wall. Ask the children to stick on the eyes, nose, and mouth, and write the captions.
- Ask the children to draw a snowman with a different hat, and write the caption 'Here is the snowman's hat'. Make the pictures into a group book.

Poems, rhymes and jingles

The snowman's song
(Tune: I'm a little teapot)
I'm a little snowman
Round and fat.
Here is my scarf,
And here is my hat.
When the snow is falling
hear me say,
'It's cold today,
And I can stay.'

I'm a little snowman
Round and fat.
Here is my scarf,
And here is my hat.
When the sun is shining
Hear me cry,
'I'm melting down.
Goodbye! Goodbye!'

Beverley Randell

Word level work	Sentence level work	Text level work	High-frequency words
to practise and secure alphabetic knowledge by helping children to self-correct over possible confusion of similar words such as 'snowman' and 'snowball'.	To encourage the use of appropriate expression by telling children to read 'like talking'.	To use phonological, contextual, grammatical and graphic knowledge to work out, predict and to make sense of what they are reading.	look, at, the, come, on, Mum, here, big, little, too, Dad

A birthday cake for Ben

Story by Beverley Randell
Illustrations by Genevieve Rees

Level: Red Set 1
Genre: Story with familiar settings
Running words: 59
Links to other PM titles: *Ben's Teddy Bear, Ben's treasure hunt, Ben's dad*

Overview
In this story about Ben's birthday cake, suspense is built into the story as the reader is encouraged to speculate on the connection between the presentation of information in the text and in the illustrations. A birthday cake for Ben will help children to develop crucial graphic and text-processing skills, as well as the importance of inference-making in reading stories.

Introducing the text
- Discuss the cover. Encourage the children to predict what the story may be about before telling them the title.
- Ensure that the children notice that Mum does not come in until Ben is asleep. Speculate on why Mum is looking at the dinosaur.
- Predict what sort of book Mum is looking at on page 9, and what she is going to make.
- Confirm predictions from the illustration on page 11.
- After looking at pages 14 and 15, make sure the links have been made between Mum looking at the dinosaur and the cake.

Reading the text
- Ensure the children notice the different endings of 'look'; 'looking' on page 4 and 'looks' on page 6.
- Notice if the children have recognised 'too' on page 6.
- Notice if the children read the 's' on 'comes' on page 6 and 's' on 'Ben's' on page 10.
- Use initial letter cues to cross-check with picture cues for accurate reading of 'tail' on page 12 and 'head' on page 13.

Revisiting the text
- Discuss how old Ben is. Find the information in the illustration on pages 14 and 15.
- Draw children's attention to the picture of Dad beside Ben's bed on page 3. Notice that Dad is not in the story. Discuss where he is by drawing children's attention to the naval uniform.
- Use magnetic letters to change 'look' into 'looks' and 'looking'.
- Can the children find a little word at the end of 'birthday'?
- Make letter strings from 'book' or 'Ben'.

Writing activities
- Write a simple recipe for Ben's cake. List the ingredients. Put in the ..., Put in the ..., Put the cake in the oven.
- Make birthday cards.
- Write about children's birthday party experiences.

Poems, rhymes and jingles

Five little candles
Five little candles
On a birthday cake;
Let's count them very carefully,
So there's no mistake.

Word level work	Sentence level work	Text level work	High-frequency words
To recognise the critical features of words.such as endings of 'look', 'looking' ,and 'looks'.	To expect reading to make sense.	To use phonological, contextual, grammatical and graphic knowledge to work out, predict and make sense of what they read.	is, up, on, the, bed, at, a, Mum, in, too, here

Baby Lamb's first drink

Story by Beverley Randell
Illustrations by Ernest Papps

Level: Red Set 2
Genre: Story with predictable language
Running words: 60
Links to other PM titles: *Hedgehog is hungry; The lazy pig* (Thematic)

Overview

Spring is here and Baby Lamb is hungry. This title could be linked with other Red level titles about seasons and animals' needs. It will also appeal to children's own sense of security. Why are baby animals born in spring? How does Mother Sheep know that Baby Lamb is hungry? What are the names of other baby animals born in the spring?

Introducing the text

- Discuss the cover picture. Read the title and discuss spring and new-born lambs.
- Discuss the picture on page 7 and the noise that Baby Lamb would make. Ask the children to find the word 'Baa'.
- Ensure that children understand that Mother Sheep is speaking on page 8.
- On page 14, ask why Baby Lamb's tail is wagging so fast.

Reading the text

- If a child reads 'here' for 'hungry' on page 6, use final letter cues to encourage self-correction.
- Use speech on page 8 to encourage the child to read 'like talking'.
- If children read 'lamb' for 'sheep', reinforce the 'sh' phoneme.

Revisiting the text

- Use the first picture to discuss the seasons.
- Discuss the ending. Why are they happy in the spring?
- Develop a word list of other words beginning like 'sheep'.
- Look at pages 14 and 16, and discover why 'Baby Lamb' is written with capital letters.

Writing opportunities

- Write a book about spring, for example:
    Spring is here.
    Piglet is here.
    Calf is here.
- Make a 'mother-and-baby' flap book, for example:
    My baby is a kitten.
    Mother Cat (written under the flap).
- Have pictures of animals with speech bubbles. Write animal noises in the speech bubbles. (Refer to *The lazy pig*.). Use these to make an interactive display.

Poems, rhymes and jingles

Spring
Little lambs in the field at play
Little birds singing songs all day
Little flowers among the grass
Tell us spring is here at last.

Word level work	Sentence level work	Text level work	High-frequency words
To recognise common spelling patterns such as words beginning like 'sheep'.	To read to make sense and to read aloud, using expression. such as use of word 'Baa'.	To describe the spring setting of the story and relate it to child's own experiences of spring.	is, here, I, am, up, for, the, look, at, and, are, in

Sally and the daisy

Story by Beverley Randell
Illustrations by Meredith Thomas

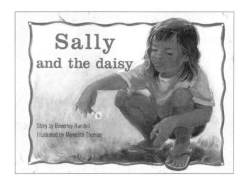

Level: Red Set 2
Genre: Story with familiar language
Running words: 60
Links to other PM titles: *Sally's beans; Sally and the sparrows; Sally's red bucket*

Overview

There are a number of learning objectives that you may wish to highlight in this text. The story shows how plants need light before they can open; it also shows the relationship between Sally and her Mum. On a phonic level, you may wish to emphasise the final 'y' sound at the end of 'Sally' and 'daisy'.

- Introduce the text.
- Remind the children who Sally is if they have read PM Starters.
- Interpret the illustrations in relation to the time of the day. Refer to previously read texts, *The lazy pig* and *Wake up, Dad*.
- Introduce pages 12 and 14 by asking what Sally might be saying.
- Ensure the children realise there is a change of speaker on page 16.

Reading the text

- Check that the high-frequency words are secure. Ask children to re-read to ensure self-correction.
- Encourage the use of punctuation on page 13 to read with expression.

Revisiting the text

- Discuss illustrations on pages 4 and 10. Notice the changes in colour and the way Sally is dressed. Discuss the time frame between the two pictures.
- Speculate where Sally might be going early in the morning.
- Make 'Sally' and 'daisy' with magnetic letters. Explore the sound 'y' makes at the end of a word.
- Use magnetic letters to change 'is' into 'it' and 'in'.

Writing activities

- Ask children to write about any presents or surprises that they have given their Mum.
- Ask the children to make the story into a simple sequence such as:
  Here is the daisy.
  Here is Sally.
  Here is the sun.
- Ask children to write a thank-you letter to Sally as if they were Sally's Mum.

Poems, rhymes and jingles

The daisy
Early in the morning
The daisy droops her head
As if to say 'I'm sleepy
And want to stay in bed.'
But when the sun is shining
She uncurls her petals small
She opens up her daisy face
And stands up straight and tall.

Word level work	Sentence level work	Text level work	High-frequency words
To hear and say phonemes in final position. Link to games outlined in 'Progression in phonics'.	To encourage use of punctuation on page 13 to read with expression.	To discuss the time frame of the story and what happened to Sally and the plant.	the, is, here, comes, can, see, the, no, up, on, look, a, Mum, for, you

The big kick

Story by Beverley Randell
Illustrations by Ernest Papps

Level: Red Set 2
Genre: Story with predictable language
Running words: 67
Links to other PM titles: *Sausages; Tom is brave; Mumps; The new baby*

Overview

Tom and his dad are playing football in their back yard when, with an almighty kick, Dad loses the ball. Note how the repetition of words is used for emphasis in this story. 'Dad kicked the ball, up , up, up' indicates the force of the kick, whereas the accumulation of the word 'looked' over pages 6-10, plus the bold emphasis, indicates the intensity of the search.

Introducing the text

- Read the title and discuss who is going to make the big kick.
- Look at the illustration on page 3 to confirm prediction and guess where the ball is going to land.
- Introduce the exclamation that Dad and Tom make.
- Use the illustration on page 11 to predict who will find the ball.
- Discuss how Tom and Dad are going to get the ball down.
- This is the first book to use 'said Tom/Dad'. Ensure the children know who is speaking.

Reading the text

- Children should read the whole text individually while the teacher reinforces known reading strategies and encourages those not yet mastered.
- Ensure that the children read the repeated word on page 2.
- Encourage the use of the phoneme 'sh' to read the new word 'shouted' on page 4.
- Check that the children notice the ending of 'looked'.
- Check that the children notice the difference between 'shouted' and 'said'.

Revisiting the text

- Use magnetic letters to revise 'look', 'looks', 'looking' and introduce 'looked'. Repeat with 'shout' or 'kick'.
- Make letter strings from 'ball' such as:
    call tall wall.
- Discuss other ways that Tom or Dad might have got the ball out of the tree.

Writing activities

- Discuss and write about the times when the children might have solved a problem at home or in the classroom, for example:
    Sarah found Jacob's writing book.
    We found Miss Jones' whistle.
- Innovate on the story to introduce position words, for example:
    Dad kicked the ball over the fence.
    He kicked the ball behind the tree.
    He kicked the ball under the bushes.
- Use the illustrations on pages 7, 9, and 11 and add speech bubbles.

Poems, rhymes and jingles

A ball
Kick a ball, chase a ball
Hit a ball too,
Toss it up and catch it
As it comes back to you.

Jenny Giles

Word level work	Sentence level work	Text level work	High-frequency words
To investigate and recognise word patterns, for example 'look', 'looked', 'looking' and 'looks'.	To look at how words are used for emphasis in the story through repetition or by bold emphasis.	To reinforce and apply their word level skills through Shared and Guided reading.	Dad, the, up, and, for, the, ball, I, can, see, tree, in, me, here, are, said, is

Sausages

Story by Beverley Randell
Illustrations by Ernest Papps

Level: Red Set 2
Genre: Story with predictable language
Running words: 79
Links to other PM titles: *The big kick; Tom is brave; Mumps; The new baby*

Overview
This is the second story about Tom. Note the similarities between the covers of this story and *The big kick*. Note also how the narrative is carried entirely by direct speech, and how this affects the story's form. You may wish to draw attention to the use of 'here' in a variety of different sentence structures.

Introducing the text
- Discuss children's experiences of barbecues.
- Read the title.
- Use the illustration on page 3 to introduce the problem and the sound 'sh-sh-sh!'.
- Predict what Dad and Tom will do.
- On page 7 use the picture cues to predict what Tom is saying.

Reading the text
- Ensure the child is reading the final 's' on sausages.
- Ensure the child is noticing the grammatical agreement, matching noun (plural) to verb (are).
- Has the child noticed the change to 'sausage' on page 10?

Revisiting the text
- Discuss the safety aspect implicit within the illustration on page 7.
- Discuss what else Dad and Tom might have decided to cook.

- Use magnetic letters to turn nouns into plurals such as 'sausages', 'matches'. Use words from other known texts such as 'horses' and 'pigs' in *The merry-go-round*.
- Use 'sh-sh-sh!' on page 2 to reinforce the 'sh' phoneme by finding other words that begin the same way.

Writing activities
- Re-write the text as a simple sequence.
  Here are the sausages.
  Here are the matches.
  Here is the fire.
- Ask the children to write a recipe for the hot dogs. On page 15, Mum comes out with the bread.
  1 sausage
  1 slice of bread
  Tomato sauce
  Roll it up
- Use the illustration on page 16, this time ask the children to use speech bubbles for the speech.

Poems, rhymes and jingles

Ten fat sausages
Ten fat sausages sizzling in a pan
One went pop and the other went bang!
Eight fat sausages sizzling in a pan
One went pop and the other went bang!
etc.

Word level work	Sentence level work	Text level work	High-frequency words
To investigate and learn spellings of words with 's' for plurals, for example 'sausages', 'horses'.	To use expression appropriate to grammar of text, being aware, for example, that the narrative of *Sausages* is entirely by direct speech.	To choose and read familiar stories. To recognise, for example the similarities between the covers of this story and *The big kick*.	Mum, is, and, I, am, said, Dad, at, the, are, in, here, you, look, a, for, to, too

Pussy and the birds

Story by Beverley Randell
Illustrations by Betty Greenhatch

Level: Red Set 2
Genre: Story with patterned language
Running words: 76
Links to other PM titles: *Tiger, Tiger; Lizard loses his tail* (Thematic)

Overview

This is an everyday story of a cat who unsuccessfully tries to catch a bird to satisfy her hunger. The story can be used in conjunction with other stories about animals' eating habits, or you could allow children to discuss their own pets' behaviour. On a phonic level, the medial 'ee' phoneme can be taught.

Introducing the text

- Discuss the cover and the children's experiences of cats.
- Introduce the story by referring to other texts the children may have read about other hungry animals. (*The lazy pig; Baby Lamb's first drink; Hedgehog is hungry; Tiger, Tiger.*) What is Pussy looking for?
- Discuss why the birds on pages 8 and 9 are looking down at Pussy and shouting.
- Predict how Pussy will solve the problem.
- On page 12, discuss where Pussy might go after she has eaten the food.

Reading the text

- Use initial letter cue and picture cue to read 'safe'.
- Ensure each child notices the 's' on 'birds' on page 9.
- Use a meaning cue to read 'miaow' on page 11.
- Use the bold type on page 15 to read with expression.
- Does each child read the speech bubbles from the top of page 16?

Revisiting the text

- Use the illustrations on page 2 or page 6 to encourage the use of descriptive vocabulary.
- Use the illustrations on pages 8 and 16 to compare how the birds felt.
- Ask the children to write as many high-frequency words from the story as they can in a given time limit.
- Make 'hungry' with magnetic letters. Revise the 'y' sound at the ends of words.
- Make 'bed' with magnetic letters. Change the medial letter 'bid', 'bad', 'bud'.
- Notice the rhyming words 'asleep' and 'cheep' at the end of the book. Make up some more rhymes for the children to finish.

Writing activities

- In a shared exercise, write a simple report using the children's knowledge about cats.
  > Cats eat meat.
  > They sleep in the day.
  > They have whiskers.
- If the children have a cat at home, ask them to write about their pet. This can be made into a wall story or zig-zag book.
- Tell the children to make a list of the things cats like to eat.
- Tell the children to make a list of the places where cats like to sleep.

Poems, rhymes and jingles

> **Pussy cat, pussy cat**
> Pussy cat, pussy cat
> Where have you been?
> I've been to London
> To visit the Queen.
>
> Pussy cat, pussy cat
> What did you there?
> I frightened a little mouse
> Under her chair.

Word level work	Sentence level work	Text level work	High-frequency words
To secure identification, spelling and reading of medial letter sounds, for example 'ee'.	To predict words from preceding words in sentences. For example, use meaning cue to read 'miaow'.	To identify and discuss characters, for example the cat. Compare with other texts about hungry animals.	is, for, a, here, up, the, tree, look, down, at, come, in, you, are, not, on, bed

The baby owls

Story by Beverley Randell
Illustrations by Elizabeth Russell-Arnot

Level: Red Set 2
Genre: Story with predictable language
Running words: 92
Links to other PM titles: *Pussy and the birds; Tiger, Tiger; Hedgehog is hungry* (Thematic)

Overview

In this story about a mother owl who goes hunting for her hungry chicks while the rest of the farm animals sleep, we see how language can be used to evoke a mood. By repeating the same sentences and words at the beginning and end of this book, the author deftly creates a quiet, still atmosphere. At the end, these serve to lull the baby owls to sleep. Although included in the story range, this text is narrative based on facts. This is a distinction you may wish to draw to your pupils' attention.

Introducing the text

- Read the title and discuss what time it must be. Discuss what the other animals would be doing.
- Ensure the children hear the phrase, 'down on the farm' from pages 2 and 14.
- Draw the children's attention to the speech bubble on page 4, and relate it to the words in italics on page 12.
- Ensure the children use the phrase 'not asleep' rather than 'awake' which may be more familiar.

Reading the text

- Check the children are noticing the final 's' on 'cows', 'pigs', 'dogs' and 'owls'.
- Encourage the children's cross-checking skills by using picture cues and initial letters to read the names of the animals on pages 2 and 14.
- Encourage the children to use the initial letter for self-correction if they read 'butterflies' for 'moths' on page 7.

Revisiting the text

- Look at the illustrations on pages 6 and 7 and discuss what else Mother Owl could have found.
- Look at page 16 and discuss why the baby owls are asleep and where Mother Owl might be.
- Get the children to list any other animals that hunt at night that they might know.
- Make a list of other words that begin with the initial phoneme 'o', like 'owl'.

Writing activities

- Re-read the text and use the illustrations to list some facts about owls.
- Ask the children to make a 'sleep/not asleep' book using their own names and names of animals they know who hunt at night.
    Rahill is asleep. Hedgehog is not asleep.
    Anthony is asleep. Owl is not asleep.
- Use one of the illustrations of Mother Owl or the baby owls to write descriptive words. Tell the children to draw a large picture and use the descriptive words to write sentences underneath.

Poems, rhymes and jingles

The owl
The owl is a nocturnal bird.
One you seldom sight.
He's busy sleeping all the day
And catching food at night.

Word level work	Sentence level work	Text level work	High-frequency words
To notice the plurals in the story with 's', for example cows, pigs, dogs, owls.	To draw attention to the speech bubble on page 4 and relate it to words in italics on page 12.	To encourage children's cross-checking skills by using picture cues and initial letters to read the names of the animals.	down, on, the, are, up, in, tree, not, look, is, for, a, big, here, to, too

The bumper cars

Story by Beverley Randell
Illustrations by Elspeth Lacey

Level: Red Set 2
Genre: Story with a familiar setting
Running words: 94
Links to other PM titles: *The photo book; Wake up, Dad; The merry-go-round; The flower girl; Hide and seek; Where are the sunhats?*

Overview

This is the fourth story so far about Kate, James, Nick and Dad. Encourage your pupils to make links between the stories. For instance, all four characters are wearing the same clothes as they are in *The merry-go-round*, so it is possible that both these stories take place during the same visit to the fair.

Introducing the text

- Read the title and discuss where you would find bumper cars.
- Infer who has first seen the bumper cars on page 3.
- Look at the illustration on page 7. Predict whether Dad will let Nick go on the bumper car.
- From the illustration on page 11, can you tell whether Nick and Dad will go on a bumper car?
- Predict how the story will end.

Reading the text

- Encourage children to use initial letter cues to read 'James' on page 2.
- Check children are noticing the final 's' on 'cars'.
- Use initial letter cues to read all the children's names on page 4.
- Check children have noticed the change from 'said' to 'shouted' on page 12. If children have read 'said', encourage self-correction by asking them to re-read and look carefully at the initial letters.

Revisiting the text

- Discuss why James and Kate went in a bumper car by themselves but Nick went with Dad.
- Discuss any rides at funfairs the children can/cannot go on and who goes with them.
- Look at the illustration on page 16 and discuss how the children and dad are feeling.
- Re-read page 14 and discuss how we read the bold text.
- Make a word string using 'car', for example 'far', 'tar', 'jar'.
- Segment and blend 'can'. Write 'can' on the board as the children say the letters.

Writing activities

- Allow the children to write about their experiences at a fun fair or theme park.
- The children may draw themselves in different coloured cars and write a caption.
    I am in the yellow car.
Make into a book or wall display.
- Use the illustration on page 15 to make a speech bubble for Dad and Nick.

Poems, rhymes and jingles

> **Bumper cars** *(Tune: Jingle bells)*
> Bumper cars, bumper cars,
> Bumping all the way.
> Oh, what fun it is to ride
> In a bumper car today.
>
> *Beverley Randell*

Word level work	Sentence level work	Text level work	High Frequency words
To secure identification, spelling and reading of initial letter sounds in simple words.	To use awareness of grammar to decipher new and unfamiliar words.	To identify and discuss the four characters and how they behave and are described in the text.	come, here, Dad, said, look, at, the, and, too, can, I, go, in, a, red, are, is, blue, we

The flower girl

Story by Jenny Giles
Illustrations by Elspeth Lacey

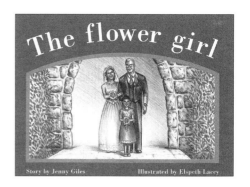

Level: Red Set 2
Genre: Story with predictable language
Running words: 90
Links to other PM titles: *The photo book; Wake up, Dad; The merry-go-round; The bumper cars; Hide and seek; Where are the sunhats?*

Overview
Your pupils may be surprised to discover that Nick is a girl whose full name is Nicola. Allow them to revisit other stories about this family to see how the confusion arose. In this story, Nick is envious of her older sister's role as flower girl. Encourage children to relate their own experiences of sibling rivalry, and what their parents did about it.

Introducing the text
- Read the title and discuss what a flower girl would do at a wedding.
- Ask your pupils to spot the characters they know on page 3. Can they see where Kate is standing? (Behind the bride and groom.)
- Discuss what Mum is saying to Nick on page 7 and notice Nick's expression. This is the first time we have seen Nick in a dress! Encourage children to give their reasons why they think Nick is cross.
- Predict why Nick wants flowers on page 11.
- Ensure the children hear Nick's full name, Nicola, on page 12 and find it in the text.
- Confirm the children's predictions on the last page.

Reading the text
- Read the text. Children will need to use the picture cues for the new vocabulary, for example: 'wedding', 'flowers'.
- Ask them to confirm the word is correct by cross-checking with initial letters.

Revisiting the text
- Discuss why Dad wanted to stop Nick on page 12. What does Nick think a flower girl is?
- Discuss what Mum and Dad might say to Nick at the end of the story.
- Decide which flower girl the story actually is about.
- Make a list of other words that begin with 'fl'.
- Make 'can' with magnetic letters and change the last letter to make new words such as 'cat', 'cap', 'cab'.
- Ask the children to write the following high-frequency words in the story in a given time limit:
    and, at, is, the, look, in, come, me, here, am

Writing activities
- Make a photo book of the wedding by getting the children to draw the sorts of pictures a photographer might have taken. Examples of captions could be:
    Here is Nick at the wedding.
    Here is Mum at the wedding.
    Here are James and Dad looking at the cars.
- Recall any incidents where the children have done something to embarrass their parents, and ask them to write a sentence about it. Turn these into a book.
- Look at the illustration on page 13 and ask the children to write down what the other guests might be saying.

Poems, rhymes and jingles

'So there!' said Nick
They said Nick wasn't old enough.
Nick said, 'It isn't fair!
I'll show them I can do it.
So there!' said Nick. 'So there!'

Word level work	Sentence level work	Text level work	High-frequency words
To learn new words from reading and shared experiences, for example words about weddings.	To predict words from preceding words.	To discuss reasons for, or causes of, incidents in stories. To discuss, for example, Nick's feelings and actions.	and, are, at, a, is, the, too, girl, look, said, Mum, can, you, see, come, and, for, me, no, Dad, here, I, am

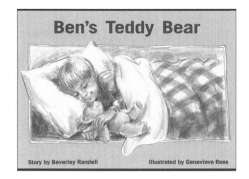

Ben's Teddy Bear

Story by Beverley Randell
Illustrations by Genevieve Rees

Level: Red Set 3
Genre: Story with predictable structure
Running words: 69
Links to other PM titles: Ben's treasure hunt; A birthday cake for Ben; Ben's dad

Overview
As will become apparent in the 'Ben' stories, the pictures play a vital role in decoding the text. Deriving meaning from the relationship between text and illustration is therefore one of the learning objectives of these stories. In this story, children should notice Teddy's leg under Ben's clothes on the chair. The story is satisfactorily resolved with Ben, now reunited with his teddy bear, going to sleep.

Introducing the text
- Read the title and relate it to the children's experiences of taking a favourite toy to bed.
- Discuss what Mum is saying on page 3, and on page 4 discuss why Ben is not in bed.
- Predict who will find Teddy. Look at the illustration on page 8 to find Teddy.
- Will Ben go to sleep when he has found Teddy?

Reading the text
- If a child has difficulty reading 'where' on page 7, look at the question mark and ask a question related to the meaning of the text.
- If a child has difficulty reading page 11, use both initial letter cues and ask a question related to the text.
- Use the punctuation and the bold print to ensure that the child is reading with expression.

Revisiting the text
- Use the illustration on the title page to encourage the use of descriptive language about teddy bears.
- Discuss why Ben takes Teddy Bear to bed.
- Discuss how Ben is feeling on page 10. Extend the children's vocabulary, using words such as 'unhappy', 'miserable'.
- Write 'Ben' with magnetic letters and change the medial vowel to make words such as 'bun', 'bin', 'ban'.
- Segment and blend 'Ben' and write the word. Repeat with 'bed'.

Writing activities
- Make a chart of the toys the children or their brothers and sisters take to bed.
- Make flap pictures with captions such as 'Where is my _____?' . 'Look _____' .
- Use the illustration on page 8 to make up sentences using position words.
    Ben is looking under the bed.
    Mum is looking between the sheets.
- Make a 'teddy bear' book.
    My teddy is soft.
    My teddy has got one eye.

Poems, rhymes and jingles

This little teddy
This little teddy likes cuddles
This little teddy likes tea
This little teddy likes hugs
Because this little teddy likes me.

He is my dear little teddy
He is my very own Ted
He is my best little teddy
And he sleeps in my little bed.

Word level work	Sentence level work	Text level work	High-frequency words
To extend vocabulary by discussing new words to describe Ben's feelings.	To use punctuation and bold print to ensure the child is reading with expression.	To recognise the relationship between text and illustration to help predict, and make sense of what the child is reading.	go, to, said, Mum, at, is, not, up, where, for, here, you, in, bed, too, are

Ben's treasure hunt

Story by Beverley Randell
Illustrations by Genevieve Rees

Level: Red Set 3
Genre: Story with predictable structure
Running words: 72
Links to other PM titles: *Ben's Teddy Bear; A birthday cake for Ben; Ben's dad*

Overview
As in *Ben's Teddy Bear*, in this next story about Ben, the reader is made to use problem-solving strategies in deriving meaning from the text. By incorporating some of the narrative material within the illustrations, the author reinforces the interdependence of text and illustration for deriving meaning.

Introducing the text
- Read the title and the clue on the cover. Discover what the children understand about a treasure hunt.
- Read the clue on the title page. Discuss what the treasure might be.
- Discuss what Mum is saying on page 2, and draw clue 1 to the children's attention but do not read it.
- Ensure the children make the relationship between Ben shouting 'A clue' and the illustrations.
- On page 13 review the predictions made when reading the title page. Revise them if necessary according to what the children now know about where the treasure will be found.

Reading the text
- Check that the children have got the pattern of the story after page 5.
- The children should read the right-hand page before reading the clue.
- The children should be using the picture cues to work out the clues.
- Check that the children notice the change on the last page from 'shouted' to 'said'.

Revisiting the text
- Create a treasure hunt in the classroom for the group.
- Discuss the children's concept of 'treasure'.

- Review the use of capital letters using the text on page 11.
- Review the recognition of high-frequency words written with both upper and lower case letters, such as 'Here/here' on page 3.

Writing activities
- Make a 'What am I?' book with clues and a picture under a flap, for example:
    I like to eat snails.
    I am a hedgehog.
- Get the children to write clues for a treasure hunt using the high-frequency words that they can read and spell, such as: 'Look on/in the _____. Ask them to draw pictures to accompany the clues.
- Make an interactive wall display with a large pirate's chest with a flap. The children could then draw treasure to go inside and write the caption: I can see _____ .

Poems, rhymes and jingles

My Treasure
I'm looking in the garden
I'm looking in the house
I'm looking round for treasure
Like a treasure-hunting mouse.

I'm looking up high
And I'm looking down low
Treasure can be anywhere
You never quite know.

I've found a speckled marble
And a shiny golden ring
An old silver pencil
And an interesting thing.

Then I took my treasure
And showed my family
They told me I could keep it
So it all belongs to me.

Jenny Giles

Word level work	Sentence level work	Text level work	High-frequency words
to read on sight high-frequency words written with both upper and lower case letters.	To review the use of capital letters for names and for the start of a sentence.	To use a range of problem-solving strategies in deriving meaning from text, such as looking at the interdependence of text and illustration in the story.	look, went, he, to, the, said, here, come, is, for, I, a, in, Mum, you, on

Lizard loses his tail

Story by Beverley Randell
Illustrations by Bruce Lauchlan

Level: Red Set 3
Genre: Story with predictable structure
Running words: 54
Links to other PM titles: *Hedgehog is hungry; The Baby Owls; Tiger, Tiger* (Thematic)

Overview

Compare and contrast this title with others in the Red level about the feeding habits of animals. Note the change in perspective between *Hedgehog is hungry* where we are pleased that hedgehog finds insects to eat, and this story where the reader is relieved when lizard escapes.

Introducing the text

- Read the title and explain that the children are going to find out how the lizard loses his tail.
- Look at the title page and discover lizard's tail. Predict what will happen to the tail.
- Refer to any previously read texts, for example: *Tiger, Tiger*, *The lazy pig* and *Sally and the daisy* where the story opens with something asleep.
- Use the word 'Kingfisher' and ensure the children understand it is the name of the bird.
- Refer to any known story, for example *Pussy and the birds* or *Tiger, Tiger* on page 11.
- Predict whether Lizard will get away (page 11). When does he lose his tail?
- Ensure the children hear the pattern 'Away goes Lizard' on page 13.

Reading the text

- Check that the children are using self-correction by asking them to re-read if a mistake is made.
- Encourage the use of cross-checking the picture cue with the initial letter if 'safe' or 'eating' is difficult.
- Encourage the use of the punctuation as a prompt if 'where' is difficult on page 15.

Revisiting the text

- Discuss the cover illustration to focus on the use of camouflage.
- Make a list of other small creatures Kingfisher might find in a garden. Refer to *Hedgehog is hungry* if the story is known.
- Find all the words in the text that end with 'ing'.
- Blend and segment 'sun'. Ask the children to write all the sounds they can hear.
- Use one of the illustrations of the Kingfisher to encourage the use of descriptive language.

Writing activities

- Innovate on *Brown Bear, Brown Bear* by Bill Martin:

    Kingfisher, Kingfisher
    What do you see?
    I see a sleepy lizard hiding from me.
    Brown lizard, brown lizard
    What do you see?
    I see a Kingfisher hunting for me.

- Re-read the story to discover some facts about lizards and demonstrate how to write a simple report.

    Lizards like to sleep in the sun.
    Lizards can lose their tails.
    Lizards hide … .

- Use the illustrations for children to write the story in their own words.

Poems, rhymes and jingles

Lazy old lizard
There's a lazy old lizard
Who lives in the zoo
He catches the flies
And swallows them too.

Word level work	Sentence level work	Text level work	High-frequency words
To recognise the critical features of words, for example common spelling patterns with 'ing' endings.	To expect reading to make sense and check if it does not.	To identify and compare basic story elements, for example, compare and contrast this story with other Red level stories about the feeding habits of animals.	he, the, where, up, here, come, is, for, home, at, in, going, away

Father Bear goes fishing

Story by Beverley Randell
Illustrations by Isabel Lowe

Level: Red Set 3
Genre: Story with a fantasy setting
Running words: 98
Links to other PM titles: *Blackberries; Baby Bear goes fishing*

Overview
The first in the Bear Family chronicles, this story introduces animals who have been endowed with anthropomorphic qualities. Note how this differs in terms of narrative style from titles such as *Baby Lamb's first drink* or *Lizard loses his tail*.

Introducing the text
- Before reading the title ask the children to predict what the story is about.
- Discuss whether real bears catch fish.
- Use 'river' when discussing the illustration on page 2.
- Discuss the expression on Father Bear's face in the illustration on page 4.
- Notice the watch that Mother Bear is consulting to guess the question she is asking.
- Discuss why they are waiting for Father Bear.

Reading the text
- Children may need to point as they read the final sentence on page 3 to ensure they do not leave out 'down'.
- If 'Where' presents a difficulty, ask the children to look at the punctuation on page 5.
- 'Home' may cause a difficulty on page 15. Ask a question related to the context, and ask the children to cross-check their answers with the initial letter.

Revisiting the text
- List the facts about bears that the children know.
- Make up an alternative ending to the story if Father Bear had not caught any fish.
- Role-play the last part of the story in groups of three.
- Look at the illustration on page 16 and allocate the fish to each bear. Ask the children the reasons for their choices.
- Make 'fish' and 'shouted' with magnetic letters. Ask the children what is the same in the two words. Make a list of other words that end with 'sh'.
- Find all the words that begin with 'f' in the story. Make up alliterative phrases.
    Four fat fish for Father Bear.

Writing activities
- Add speech bubbles to the illustration on page 10 to continue the converstion between Mother Bear and Baby Bear.
- Ask the children to write about their own experiences of going fishing.
- Write instructions on how to cook the fish:
    1 fish
    Some butter
    Put the fish in a pan
    Cook it
- Children write their own version of the story in sequence.

Poems, rhymes and jingles

One, two, three, four, five
One, two, three, four, five
Once I caught a fish alive
Six, seven, eight, nine, ten
Then I let it go again.

Why did you let it go?
Because it bit my finger so.
Which little finger did it bite?
This little finger on the right.

Word level work	Sentence level work	Text level work	High-frequency words
To secure identification, spelling and reading of initial, finer and medial letter sounds in simple words.	To predict words from preceding words in sentences.	To reinforce and apply their word-level skills through Shared and Guided Reading.	went, he, down, to, the, where, are, said, up, here, come, is, and, for, I, am, home, at, a, me

Tom is brave

Story by Beverley Randell
Illustrations by Ernest Papps

Level: Red Set 3
Genre: Story with a familiar setting
Running words: 57
Links to other PM titles: *The big kick; Sausages; Mumps; The new baby*

Overview

This story about Tom could be used during PSHE to talk about safety or citizenship issues. What could someone have done if they had seen Tom fall over? When is it safe to go shopping on one's own? Why did Tom's mum wash his wound?

Introducing the text

- Discuss the children's own experiences of hurting themselves before reading the title.
- Discuss what being brave means.
- On page 5, draw attention to the fact that Tom is not watching where he is going.
- Ensure the children understand that they, as readers, are warning Tom to look where he is going.
- Predict what is going to happen.
- Discuss the expression on Tom's face on page 15. Why does he want everyone to look at him?

Reading the text

- Check if the children use the bold print to read with expression.
- On page 10 the children should use picture cues to read the text.
- Check that the children read both words in the compound word 'into' on page 14.

Revisiting the text

- Look at the illustration on page 13 to discuss what Mum has done to Tom's knees.
- Revisit page 5 and elaborate on why Tom is not looking where he is going.
- Discuss safety in the home or at school.
- Make 'look' with magnetic letters and add 'ing' and 'ed'. Repeat the exercise with 'go'. Ask the children if we say 'goed'? Can they find the word we do use on page 2 or page 10?
- Make 'in' and 'to' with magnetic letters and join them into a compound word. Ask the children to see if they can find 'into' in another book (such as the big book).

Writing activities

- Ask the children to write a shopping list for Tom to take to the shops.
- Write the list into a story innovating on *Don't forget the bacon* by Pat Hutchins:
    1 packet of crisps.
    2 red apples.
    1 bottle of milk.
    And don't forget the eggs.
- Write about children's own experiences of going shopping where something may have gone wrong.
- Ask the children to make a sign to warn other people about the paving stone.

Poems, rhymes and jingles

My Sore Knee
When I fall
And hurt my knee
Mum's the one
Who fixes me.

Beverley Randell

Word level work	Sentence level work	Text level work	High-frequency words
To read on sight approximately 30 more high-frequency words.	To read with expression, recognising, for example, use of bold print for exclamation.	To discuss reasons for, or causes of, incidents in the story about Tom.	went, he, to, the, where, the, are, said, here, and, for, I, am, home, at, me, going, Mum, home

Hide and seek

Story by Jenny Giles
Illustrations by Elspeth Lacey

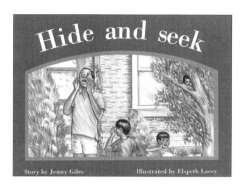

Level: Red Set 3
Genre: Story with a familiar setting
Running words: 108
Links to other PM titles: The photo book; Wake up, Dad; The merry-go-round; The bumper cars; The flower girl; Where are the sunhats?

Overview
In this book about a game of hide and seek, fictional time and real time run in parallel. Using ellipses to show Dad's counting spans several pages, the author builds suspense as we see each child hiding. Ensure that your pupils understand this convention of indicating time.

Introducing the text
- Discuss the picture on the cover and relate to children's experiences playing hide and seek.
- Remind children of the characters' names.
- Alert children to the ellipsis (...) on page 2, which means the sentence isn't finished, and that Dad carries on counting on subsequent pages.
- On page 14, discuss what Dad is shouting. Ensure the children hear or use the phrase 'you win'.

Reading the text
- The faces of the hiding children are not clear. Each child will need to use initial letter cues to check that he/she is reading the names of the children correctly.
- Check the children are noticing the change of preposition (page 8 'in', page 10 'at').
- If a child has difficulty with 'win' (page 14), use the rhyme 'in' and add the onset 'w'.

Revisiting the text
- Discuss where James and Nick could have hidden.
- Revisit the illustrations on pages 13 and 15, and discuss whether the two boys knew where Kate was hiding.
- Segment and blend 'can'. Ask the children to write the word. Repeat using 'hid' and 'box'.
- Make 'hid' with magnetic letters. Change the final consonant to make new words 'hit', 'his', 'him'.

Writing activities
- Make a wall display with flap pictures. The children draw themselves to hide under the flaps and write a caption for their picture.
    Luke hid under the table.
    Molly hid behind the TV.
- Write recounts of children's experiences of playing hide and seek. Plan using a writing frame.
    Who? (was playing) Where? (did you hide)
- Children can draw or write one word on the plan before writing one or two sentences.
- Write another page for the text where Dad goes to hide.

Poems, rhymes and jingles

Hiding (verses 1, 2, 6, 7, 8 only)
I'm hiding, I'm hiding,
And no-one knows where;
For all they can see is my
Toes and my hair.

And I just heard my father
Say to my mother –
'But, darling, he MUST be
Somewhere or other.'

'We've hunted,' sighed Mother,
'As hard as we could
And I AM afraid that we've
Lost him for good.'

Then I laughed out aloud
And wiggled my toes
And Father said – 'Look, dear,
I wonder if those

Toes could be Benny's?
There are ten of them. See?
And they were so surprised to find
Out it was me!

Dorothy Aldis

Word level work	Sentence level work	Text level work	High-frequency words
To secure identification, spelling and reading of initial, final and medial letter sounds in simple words.	To expect reading to make sense and check if it does not.	By highlighting the ellipses, to encourage the children to notice differences between written and spoken forms of writing.	see, Dad, look, he, the, where, are, said, up, here, come, is, and, I, am, at, in, you, on, tree

A home for Little Teddy

Story by Beverley Randell
Illustrations by Chantal Stewart

Level: Red Set 3
Genre: Story with patterned language
Running words: 153
Links to other PM titles: *Ben's Teddy Bear; The photo book; A roof and a door* (Thematic)

Overview
This is a story of wanting to belong somewhere. Little Teddy goes from home to home looking for a place to stay. Finally, he is invited to live in the dolls' house. This could be used as a discussion on different kinds of homes, or as a citizenship topic.

Introducing the text
- Read the title but use the illustration on page 3 to discuss why Little Teddy wants to find a home.
- Make predictions throughout the story about whether the animals will let Little Teddy come in.
- On page 12, predict whether the dolls will let Little Teddy come in. Ask the children to give reasons for their predictions.

Reading the text
- Check the children have noticed the change from 'Little Teddy' to the pronoun 'he' on page 4.
- Check the children have noticed the plural for 'mouse' on page 6.
- Check the children are reading the plurals 'rabbits' and 'dolls'.

Revisiting the text
- Draw the children's attention to Little Teddy's bag and the letters written on it.
- Discuss why the dolls' house was a good place for a Little Teddy.
- Discuss how the children felt when Little Teddy could not find a place to sleep.

- Ask the children to find words in the text that are written with upper and lower case initial letters.
    'little', 'this', 'come', 'can'
- Make a list of words that end like 'doll' with the double 'l':
    small call hall

Writing activities
- Tell the children to write another page for the story where Little Teddy asks someone else before he asks the dolls.
- Demonstrate how to write a poem about Teddy Bears, using adjectives such as:
    small bears
    tall bears
    short bears
    fat bears
    big bears
    little bears
    I like teddy bears.
- Ask them to write a response to the story:
    I felt _____ when he went to see the rabbit.
    I felt _____ when he went to see the dolls.

Poems, rhymes and jingles

Teddy bears' picnic
If you go down to the woods today,
You're in for a big surprise.
If you go down to the woods today,
You'd better go in disguise!
For every bear that ever there was
Will gather there for certain because
Today's the day the Teddy Bears have their picnic.

John Bratton and Jimmy Kennedy

Word level work	Sentence level work	Text level work	High-frequency words
To investigate and learn spellings of words with 's' for plurals, for example 'rabbits' and 'dolls' and the irregular plural 'mice'.	To expect reading to make sense and check if it does not.	To use some of the elements in the story to write another page where Little Teddy asks someone else before the dolls.	I, can, not, here, said, little, where, went, to, look, for, a, home, he, see, the, come, in, am, you, this, is, away, no, up, bed, good

Where is Hannah?

Story by Annette Smith
Illustrations by Priscilla Cutter

Level: Red Set 3
Genre: Story with a predictable setting
Running words: 142
Links to other PM titles: None

Overview
The last of the Red level storybooks, *Where is Hannah?* offers your pupils the opportunity to explore new vocabulary supported by strong clear picture cues. Children who have worked through the Red Sets will have had frequent exposure to all the high-frequency words found in the NLS Reception list, and should be reading at least 95% of these with confidence.

Introducing the text
- Read the title and predict what the story is going to be about. Discuss where the story is set.
- On page 3, confirm the children's predictions by reading the sign on the door.
- Use the word 'trampoline' on page 6, and ask the children to find the word in the story. Ask how they know it says trampoline.
- Ask the children if Mum will see Hannah. How will she find her?

Reading the text
- Children can confirm their reading on page 4 with picture cues and initial letters.
- If 'swing' is a difficult word, use meaning cues and cross-check with the initial sound 'sw'.
- There are no picture cues for 'rope' and 'trampoline' on page 12. Children could use initial letter cues and then refer back to page 4 to cross-check.

Revisiting the text
- Discuss why Hannah is always safe at the gym.
- Discuss what activities the children like best when they do PE in the hall.

- Discuss what after-school activities the children may have joined.
- Make a letter string from 'swing'. Ensure the children notice that two letters have to be removed before making new words.
- Make a list of words that start with 'sw'.
- Make a list of words that start with 'tr'.

Writing activities
- Ask children to draw pictures with captions to make a 'PE book' about themselves. For instance, Come and look at me on the _____ .
- Write an action poem. Ask the children for action words first and write on cards. On a large sheet of paper, write 'I' down the page and ask children to put on the cards they want. They can then write their own poems.
  I swing
  I jump
  I climb
  I hop
  And I roll.
- Ask the children to write a sequel about Hannah's next trip to the gym.

Poems, rhymes and jingles

In the gym
I'm bouncing on the trampoline:
Spring! Spring! Spring!
I'm clinging to the swinging rope:
Swing! Swing! Swing!

Beverley Randell

Word level work	Sentence level work	Text level work	High-frequency words
To discriminate, read and spell words with initial consonant clusters, for example 'sw'.	To use awareness of grammar of a sentence to decipher new and unfamiliar words, for example 'trampoline' and 'rope'.	To reinforce and apply their word level skills through Shared and Guided Rreading.	and, Mum, went, to, the, look, said, I, can, see, a, at, come, go, up, down, on, me, away, where, here, am, way

Eggs for Breakfast

Story by Annette Smith
Photography by John Pettitt

Level: Red Set non-fiction, 'Maths around us'
Genre: Story with information
Running words: 127
Links to other PM titles: Other Red non-fiction titles

Overview

Bearing in mind the increased difficulty of these texts, you may wish to delay your pupils' reading of the non-fiction titles as independent readers until they have worked through most of the Red Set storybooks. The non-fiction titles present information in the form of factual captions. There is a narrative link between the frames; in this case the story is narrated by a young girl who introduces us to her mother, father and younger brother around the kitchen table. The title may also be used to practise the language of number, such as 'next to', 'equals', 'the same as'.

Introducing the text

- Read the title and discuss what the children like for breakfast.
- Discuss the number in the family and how many plates, spoons and so on they would need to put on the table.
- Look at page 3. Discuss who is telling this story and what the girl is going to do.
- Discuss what she will call each family member, introducing the word 'brother'.
- Look at page 7. Discuss where each plate goes and predict what the girl will get out next.
- Look at page 11. Discuss what the girl has put on the bench and what it might be for.

Reading the text

- Each page begins differently. Check that each child reads the high-frequency words 'here', 'this', 'we' without hesitation.
- If 'mat' is an unfamiliar word direct the child to noticing 'at'.
- Check that the children are using picture cues for unfamiliar nouns (for example, spoon, plate) and cross-checking, using initial letters.
- Check the children have noticed 'an' and are not reading 'a' on pages 14 and 15.

Revisiting the text

- Compare this story to *Goldilocks and the Three Bears*. Discuss how many mats, plates, spoons and so on that the three bears would need. How many would be needed if Goldilocks came to breakfast too?
- On page 11, count the number of eggs and decide how many more egg cups the girl needs to get.
- Count the number of glasses of juice Dad has poured. How many more will he need?
- Make a list of other nouns beginning with 'e' where we need 'an'. Discuss if we use 'an' for any other letter.
- Make 'go' with magnetic letters, add 'ing' and point out we have to add 'es'.

Writing activities

- Make a list of family members:
    Marcus has one sister.
    Felix has two brothers and three sisters.
  Ask each child to write about his/her own family.
- Make a book about four of something:
    A table has four legs.
    Luke has four brothers.
- Write a wall story or book 'What we like for breakfast':
    We like eggs for breakfast.
    We like cornflakes for breakfast.
- Write a shopping list for breakfast, for example:
    bread
    butter
    cocopops
    milk

Word level work	Sentence level work	Text level work	High-frequency words
In Guided Reading to read on sight high-frequency words such as 'here', 'this', 'we' without hesitation.	To expect reading to make sense and check if it does not.	To identify and discuss the family in the story	here, is, my, we, are, to, have, this, Mum, Dad, and, the, on, me, a, an, like, for

Red and Blue and Yellow

Story by Annette Smith
Photography by John Pettitt

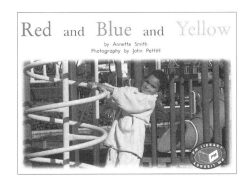

Level: Red Set non-fiction, 'Maths around us'
Genre: Story with information
Running words: 98
Links to other PM titles: Other Red non-fiction titles; *The bumper cars* (Thematic)

Overview

This title introduces the concept of colour in the world around us. Use it as a springboard to talk about colours in the classroom, and how they can be sorted into groups. What are other criteria for sorting objects? How many objects of each colour are there in the story? How many altogether? Also look at non-fiction devices, such as who is telling the story; what settings the story covers; the ways in which this story is similar to *Eggs for Breakfast* (the narrative voice).

Introducing the text

- Read the title and discuss things that are usually blue, red and yellow.
- Look at page 2. Discuss what the cars do when the lights go red, and notice what the boy and his father are doing.
- Look at page 10. Ensure that the children have heard the word 'chicks' and found it in the text.
- Identify all the colours on the school bag and in the final picture.

Reading the text

Each page begins with a high-frequency word (except page 10). Check the child is reading these fluently.
- 'Little' at the beginning of page 10 may cause difficulty. Ask the child to get ready to say the first letter and think about the size of the chicks.
- Check the child reads both 'school' and 'bag' on page 14. If 'school' is missed out, asked the child to re-read and check he/she is reading all the words.

Revisiting the text

- Revisit the illustrations and find other things in the pictures that are red, blue or yellow that are not mentioned in the text.
- Look at the illustration on page 10, and explore the children's knowledge about chickens.
- Make a graph of the children's favourite colour. The children could also ask someone else in the class as well.
- Make a rhyming string from 'red', for example:
    fed, bed, said, led, dead, head.
- Investigate which spelling pattern has the most number of words.
- Segment and blend the word 'red'. Ask the children to write the word after hearing all the sounds. Repeat with 'bed' or 'fed'.

Writing activities

- Make a 'colour' book modelled on page 5. Use a cut-out picture on the left and the child's drawing on the right.
- Make a wall display of a colour with each child writing a caption, such as:
    A pear is yellow.
    A banana is yellow.
    or
    a yellow pear
    a yellow banana
- Make a 'favourite colour' book:
    I like _____.
    Here I am in a ____ _____ (dress, coat, jumper, etc.)]
Each child contributes a page.
- Speculate on where the boy might be going on page 15. Ask the children to make a list of the things the boy might have in his bag.

Word level work	Sentence level work	Text level work	High Frequency words
To recognise common spelling patterns by making rhyming strings, for example from 'red'.	To predict text from the grammar, Re-read and check the child is reading all the words, for example 'school' and 'bag'.	To identify and discuss the style of non-fiction texts, for example, who is telling the story, the settings, the style of narrative.	at, the, go, red, and, here, is my, too, this, blue, little, yellow, school, I, can, see, all, me

Look Up, Look Down

Story by Annette Smith
Photography by John Pettitt

Level: Red Set; non-fiction
Genre: Story with information
Running words: 165
Links to other PM titles: *Ben's treasure hunt* (Thematic); *Ben's teddy bear* (Thematic); Other Red non-fiction titles

Overview

This text could be compared and contrasted with *Ben's treasure hunt*, which used a similar narrative device. Unlike the preceding non-fiction texts, this divides the narrative between four children. Ensure that your pupils are aware of this. This text also deviates from the use of factual captions. Instead, it offers a realistic recount of an event. Ask your children to retell the story, using words such as 'first', and 'then', 'next', and 'finally'. (You could structure this as a writing frame.) Use this text to reinforce prepositional language such as 'inside', 'on top of', 'under', and so on.

Introducing the text

- Read the title. Ask the children what other book they have read where the character had to look in different places.
- Remind the children about clues.
- Discuss what the children might be hunting. Ensure that they find 'teddy bear' in the text.
- Ensure the children understand the pattern of the story: first page look up, next page look down.
- Ensure the children understand the repetitive phrases in the clues.
- Ensure the children understand the pattern of the clues of hunting first in the garden and then in the house.

Reading the text

- Encourage the child to read page 2 using the rhythm like a chant or song. Re-read if necessary.
- Observe whether the child is using the bold print to read with expression.
- Encourage the children to read page 16, using the rhythm of the text.
- Observe that the children read the text changes on pages 12, 13, 14, and 15 accurately.

Revisiting the text

- Return to page 16. Discuss how the children know that all the teddy bears have been found.
- On page 5 notice the teddy bear border. Note that it continues on each clue card. Compare to *Ben's treasure hunt* and discuss why Ben's clues have no border.
- Make 'into' with magnetic letters. Note how 'in' and 'to' are separate words.
- Revise words that begin with the same initial cluster as 'chair'.
- Make a list of words beginning with the same initial cluster as 'swing'.

Writing activities

- Get the children to make bear finger-puppets and hide them in the classroom. Get the children to write clues about their own puppets and give them to another child to read and hunt for the teddy bear, for example:
    Can you find my teddy bear? Look ….
- Make a flap book of clues. Get the children to lift the flap with a picture drawn on it of the place the teddy bear is hidden. The same picture with a teddy bear is drawn underneath, for example:
    Can you find Ahmed's teddy bear?
    He is up on the teacher's table.
- Make an 'up' book, for example:
    A plane can go up.
    A kite can go up.
    A balloon can go up.
- Make a 'down' book, for example:
    I can sit down.
    I can lie down.
    I can walk down steps.

Word level work	Sentence level work	Text level work	High-frequency words
To investigate and revise words with initial consonant clusters, for example 'sw' and 'ch'.	To read with expression using the bold print as a cue.	To re-tell the story using the words 'first', 'then', 'next', and 'finally'. Look at the main points in sequence.	we, are, on, a, this, is, my, can, you, go, out, to, the, up, house, down, in, here, see, all, went, look

A Roof and a Door

Story by Annette Smith
Photography by John Pettitt

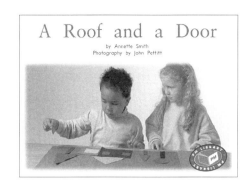

Level: Red Set non-fiction, 'Maths around us'
Genre: Story with information
Running words: 89
Links to other PM titles: Other Red non-fiction titles

Overview
The structure of this text is more complex than that of previous texts. Ensure that your pupils are aware of the changes in narrative voice. This text emphasises the recognition of geometrical shapes in the world around us. Encourage pupils to use the appropriate vocabulary for the shapes shown, and ask them to define them according to accepted criteria. Encourage them to describe the world around them in terms of shapes and patterns.

Introducing the text
- Read the title and discuss where the children live. Tell the children that the two children in this story live in different houses – a bungalow and a house with a garden.
- Ensure that the children understand that the girl is talking from pages 2 to 8 and the boy from pages 10 to 16.
- On page 8, relate the symbols to the picture on page 9 so the children identify the words 'roof', 'window', 'door', and 'path.'

Reading the text
- Observe whether the child is cross-checking picture cues with initial letters on pages 4, 5, and 8.
- Observe whether the child reads fluently, using the bold print for emphasis.
- Observe whether the child reads the different high-frequency words at the beginning of each sentence fluently.

Responding the text
- Look at the illustration on page 7. Discuss what the yellow square is going to be. Look on page 9 at the finished house to confirm.
- Use the illustration on page 16 to identify the different shapes.
- Discuss what shapes the children would use to make pictures of their houses.
- Look at the word 'path' on page 8. Make a list of other words that end with 'th'.

Writing activities
- Make a house from shapes for the wall. Ask the children to make labels, for example:
    Here is the ———.
- Make a 'house' book, for example:
    Rachel lives in a flat.
    Aaron lives in a house.
    Michelle lives in a house with a garden.
- Make a 'shape' book, for example:
    Aaron saw this wheel. He said it looks like a circle.

Word level work	Sentence level work	Text level work	High-frequency words
To read and spell words with final consonant clusters, for example 'th'.	To check if the child reads fluently using bold print for emphasis.	To use a variety of cues to work out, predict and check the meanings of unfamiliar words in the story.	this, is, our, house, the, like, my, here, a, up, to, come, and, see, look, can, you

Tall Things

Story by Annette Smith
Photography by John Pettitt

Level: Red Set non-fiction, 'Maths around us'
Genre: Story with information
Running words: 83
Links to other PM titles: Other Red non-fiction titles

Overview

Again, this title reinforces pupils' use of and exposure to comparative terminology such as 'taller than', 'shorter than', 'the same size as' by putting them in the familiar context of their everyday world. The layout of the book (portrait, not landscape like the others) complements the subject, and allows the dimension of size to be reflected. Note the distinction between empirical facts ('My teddy bear is not tall like me') and subjective opinion ('My dad is tall'). If possible, introduce the children to the distinction between fact and opinion with reference to this text.

Introducing the text

- Explore the concept of 'tall' by finding who is the tallest in the group. Find something in the environment that is taller than the children.
- Encourage the children to talk about their experiences of looking up at tall things.
- Read the title and discuss what tall things might be in the book. Notice the shape of the book.
- Ensure the children have heard and used the names of the tall things used in the text.
- Discuss skyscrapers and why the one on page 9 is as tall as the girl.
- Discuss the change on page 10 where the teddy bear is 'not tall'.
- Discuss how the girl is measuring herself against her mum and dad on pages 13 and 15.

Reading the text

- Check that each child has noticed the repetitious sentence.
- Check the accuracy of the reading because each page changes after the first sentence.
- Encourage re-reading for self-correction.
- Encourage self-correction using high-frequency words.

Revisiting the text

- Discuss what else could have been put in the book.
- Discuss family members who are tall.
- Find things in the classroom that are not tall, like the teddy bear.
- Make word strings from 'things'. Ensure the children notice that 'th' is one phoneme and therefore both letters get taken away before adding another initial sound.
- Find other words that start with the same initial letter cluster, such as '<u>cr</u>ane'.

Writing activities

- Make a comparison chart or book using the children themselves for the comparisons.
  Erica is taller than Marcus.
- Ask them to write a sentence based on page 10:
  My cat is not tall like me.
  My doll is not tall like me.
- Ask the children what they would like to do when they are tall. Make a writing frame for the children to compose their own sentence based on page 16.
  One day _____
  like _____ .
  I want to _____ .
- Ask the children to write a comparison book about what they could do when they were small and what they can do now that they are tall.

Word level work	Sentence level work	Text level work	High-frequency words
To make words strings using words such as 'things' and 'crane'.	To encourage re-reading for self-correction and for text to make sense.	To discuss reasons why various objects or people are tall or small in the book. Note shape of book.	I, look, up, at, the, are, like, a, is, too, to, my, am, not, me, dad, come, here, on, tall, one, day, will, be, and

Two Eyes, Two Ears

Story by Annette Smith
Photography by John Pettitt

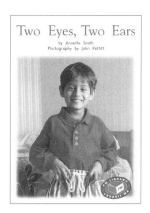

Level: Red Set non-fiction, 'Maths around us'
Genre: Story with information
Running words: 83
Links to other PM titles: Other Red non-fiction titles

Overview
This text could be used to reinforce mathematical relationships. We have two hands and arms, and two sleeves. Ask what would happen if there were three sleeves, or only one? Talk about the symmetry of the human form, and categorise the parts of the body into groups. (Two hands, two arms, but only one head.) Ensure that pupils understand that numbers can be represented as numerical figures or words, and when each is appropriate.

Introducing the text
- Ask the children to look in a mirror, or study each other, to see what they can see one of (for example, one nose, or one mouth), and what they can see two of: (two eyes, two ears, two hands).
- Note on page 5 that the boy is looking in the mirror and is counting his features.
- On page 6 he is drying himself, and he uses two arms and two hands.
- On pages 9 to 13 he is dressing himself and the text refers to sleeves, socks and shoes. Ensure the children hear these words. In particular, discuss sleeves if it is new vocabulary for the children.

Reading the text
- Look at page 6. Observe whether the children are using the picture cues, and cross-checking with initial letter cues to read hands and arms accurately.
- Observe if the children read socks and shoes accurately on page 12. If incorrect, encourage self-correction by asking the child to re-read the sentence looking carefully for the 's' or 'sh' sound.

Revisiting the text
- Discuss what is meant by twins. Ask the children why the twins were part of a book called *Two Eyes, Two Ears*.
- Look at page 10. Discuss why the boy didn't talk about putting on his shorts. (We say 'a pair of shorts' but 'two trouser legs'.)
- Make 'this' with magnetic letters. Ask the children what they notice (the little word 'is'). Ask the children to write the word without copying. Repeat several times.
- Make a list of words beginning with the same initial consonant cluster as sleeves.

Writing activities
- Make a 'two' book, for example:
    Rachel has two brothers.
    Kim has two cats.
- Draw a body shape for the wall and ask the children to write labels, for example:
    We have two arms.
- Make a 'brother' book, for example:
    This is my brother. He likes …
    This is my mum's brother. He likes …

Word level work	Sentence level work	Text level work	High-frequency words
To look at new words from reading and shared experiences through the story subject of clothes and the body.	To use picture cues and cross-checking of letter cues to read words such as 'hands' and 'arms' accurately.	To identify and discuss the boy and his actions.	look, at, me, I, and, can, see, two, and, a, with, have, here, are, for, my, this, is, he, like, we

Where are the sunhats?

Story by Beverley Randell
Illustrations by Elspeth Lacey

Level: Yellow Set 1
Genre: Story with predictable language
Running words: 130
Links to other PM titles: *The photo book; Wake up, Dad; The merry-go-round; The bumper cars; The flower girl; Hide and seek*

Overview

This is the last title in the mini-series about James, Kate, and Nick. The family is on its way to the beach when Mum remembers that they have forgotten their sunhats. You may wish to link this title to a PSHE lesson about the importance of looking after oneself in the sun. Alternatively, you could build character profiles of the children, based on the knowledge accumulated whilst reading through the previous titles.

Introducing the text

- Read the title and discuss where the family would be going and why they need sunhats. Discuss what would happen if they forgot to put the sunhats in the car.
- Look at page 5. Look at the tyre marks on the road where Dad has braked. Discuss why they have to return home.
- Look at page 10. Predict where Dad's sunhat will be and who will find it.
- Confirm predictions on pages 12 to 14.

Reading the text

- Observe whether the children use the pictures in the text on page 2 to make a sentence.
- Observe what strategies the children use to read 'where' on page 2. Encourage the children to use the punctuation or find the word on the cover.
- On page 6, ensure that the children read the compound word 'inside' and not just the first part 'in'. Encourage re-reading for self-correction.
- Encourage children to use the punctuation to read with expression.

Revisiting the text

- Discuss the type of hats your children wear in the sun. Use the illustrations to describe the family's sunhats.
- Discuss people who wear hats for a specific purpose, for example, a fireman wears a hat to a fire, a policeman wears a hat, a builder wears a hard hat. Make an illustrated chart of all the types of hat mentioned.
- List other compound words that have 'sun', for example:
    sunscreen sunshine sunburn sunlight
- List other words that end with the same consonant cluster as 'beach'.

Writing activities

- Change 'sunhats' to 'woolly hats' and then ask the children to rewrite the story where necessary.
- Ask the children to write a list of things to pack before going to the beach or the pool.
- The children could write a persuasive text on why people should wear sunhats. Provide a writing frame, along the lines of:
    People should wear _____ when _____ because _____ .

Poems, rhymes and jingles

A shady hat
A shady hat
is on my head
to stop my nose
from getting red.
Beverley Randell

Word level work	Sentence level work	Text level work	High-frequency words
To recognise compound words and list a variety connected to the text, for example 'inside', and compound words that have 'sun'.	To use punctuation in a sentence to decipher new or unfamiliar words, for example the strategies the child uses to read 'where' on page 2.	To build character profiles of the children based on the knowledge collected whilst reading the other titles about the family.	the, and, are, in, where, they, going, Dad, Mum, come, on, home, went, we, go, to, look, for, said, here, is, my, at, no, up, down, you, away

Blackberries

Story by Beverley Randell
Illustrations by Isabel Lowe

Level: Yellow Set 1
Genre: Story with elements of fantasy
Running words: 108
Links to other PM titles: *Father Bear goes fishing; Baby Bear goes fishing*

Overview

The second of the Bear family stories sees them going blackberry picking. Note how the story echoes another better known bear story (*Goldilocks and the Three Bears*) on page 5 where we are shown the different basket sizes for Father Bear, Mother Bear and Baby Bear. Compare and contrast the Bear family with other animal and non-animal families, using the non-fiction titles, if possible. Alternatively, this could be used in conjuction with the 'Maths around us' non-fiction set to talk about different sizes.

Introducing the text

- Read the title and explain how blackberries grow on prickly bushes. Ensure the children have a concept of picking fruit in the country.
- Ensure the children have understood 'basket', can locate the word in the text, and can relate it to the picture.
- Notice the worried looks on the faces of Mother Bear and Father Bear on page 8.
- Ensure the children understand what has happened to Baby Bear's blackberries.

Reading the text

- Observe the children's use of picture cues on page 5.
- Encourage the children to notice the question marks on page 9 in order to read accurately.
- Observe whether the child notices the change from 'said' to 'shouted' on page 11. Encourage self-correction.
- Encourage the use of picture cues and the high-frequency word 'in' to read 'inside' on page 16.

Revisiting the text

- Discuss times when the children have been out of sight in a shop or park.
- Look at the illustration on page 16 and decide what Mother Bear and Father Bear would say next.
- Play a version of hangman with the group. Draw a mouse with no whiskers, a rubbish bin and the lines for the letters. Give the children the first letter of the word. They must guess the second letter and give a word that would have that letter combination. For example, if the first letter were 'h' the second letter could be 'a' as in 'have' or 'i' as in 'hive'. If the child is wrong the mouse gets a whisker. If the next letter given is not a letter combination in English, the letter goes in the rubbish bin. (For example 'hg' is not a possible letter combination in English.) Repeat with each letter in order.
- Make a list of other words which begin with the same initial consonant cluster as 'blackberries'.

Writing activities

- Using the illustration on page 8, ask the children to add speech bubbles.
- Ask children to draw their favourite fruit for a wall display with captions, for example:
    I like apples because they are crunchy.
- Ask children to write their own jingles using the same pattern but changing the last line or the second and fourth line.

Word level work	Sentence level work	Text level work	High-frequency words
To use through reading and spelling initial, final and medial letter sounds in simple words using games such as hangman.	To notice the question marks in the text to help the child read accurately.	To compare and contrast the Bear family to other animal or non-animal families that appear in other titles.	and, went, to, look, for, into, this, I, like, said, where, is, are, you, after, no, he, here, I, am, in, your, me

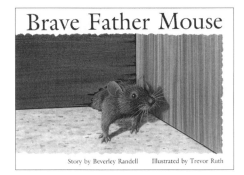

Brave Father Mouse

Story by Beverley Randell
Illustrations by Trevor Ruth

Level: Yellow Set 1
Genre: Story with predictable structure
Running words: 91
Links to other PM titles: *Tiger, Tiger; Baby Hippo* (Thematic)

Overview

Brave Father Mouse is a cleverly constructed story which ensures that the readers' sympathies lie with the hungry mouse, not the equally hungry cat. Consider how the perspective might have been changed had the title instead been 'The hungry cat'. Ensure that your pupils are aware of the way in which tension is built up by comparing and contrasting this story with those in which our sympathies lie with the hungry cat (for example, *The hungry kitten*). Explore how the incident occurred by looking at the sequence of events.

Introducing the text

- Read the title and discuss the concept of 'brave'.
- Predict what Father Mouse is going to do.
- Ensure the children realise why Father Mouse is venturing out of the hole.
- On page 8 predict what will happen.

Reading the text

- Observe whether the children notice the final 's' on the words 'wakes' and 'comes' on page 8.
- Observe how the children attempt 'downstairs' on page 8. Encourage cross-checking of picture cues with letter cues.
- Encourage the child to use the build-up of tension in the story to read expressively.

Revisiting the text

- Discuss how Father Mouse felt when he saw the cat. Discuss situations that have made the children feel scared.
- Role-play the story in groups of three.

- Make a list of words beginning with the same initial consonant cluster as 'bread'.
- Find all the compound words in the story, such as: upstairs, downstairs, away, asleep.
- What do the illustrations say about the kind of house in which the story takes place? Is it a new house? What about the people who live there?

Writing activities

- Ask the children to rewrite the story as a comic strip, making a sequence of four pictures.
- Using the illustrations, the children could write a description of mice.
- Using this writing frame as a prompt, ask the children to write a recount of an event that scared them.
    I'm scared when …
    so I …

Poems, rhymes and jingles

Mice
I think mice
Are rather nice
Their tails are long
Their faces are small
They haven't any
Chins at all.

Their ears are pink
Their teeth are white
They run about
The house at night.

They nibble things
They shouldn't touch
And no-one seems
To like them much.

But I think mice are nice.
Rose Fyleman

Word level work	Sentence level work	Text level work	High-frequency words
To discriminate, read and spell words with the initial consonant cluster of 'br', for example 'bread', 'brave'.	To use the build-up of tension in the story to read expressively.	By looking at the sequence of events to discuss the reasons and causes why the reader's sympathies lie with the mouse and not the cat.	is, after, the, cat, up, and, too, he, for, a, look, at, home, in, no, away, here

Mumps

Story by Beverley Randell
Illustrations by Ernest Papps

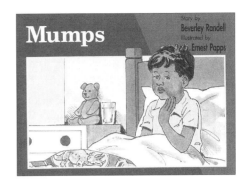

Level: Yellow Set 1
Genre: Story with predictable language
Running words: 107
Links to other PM titles: *The big kick; Sausages; Tom is brave; The new baby*

Overview
This story about Tom is written in the form of a simple diary, with events recorded on a day-by-day basis over five days. This allows us to follow the progression of Tom's illness from start to recovery. Ensure that children use their prior knowledge of Tom's character culled from previous titles to decide whether his behaviour at the beginning of the story is typical.

Introducing the text
- Look at the picture on the cover and discuss if any children have been sick like that. Read the title.
- Ensure the children understand how miserable Tom feels on page 3.
- Ensure the children understand the sequence of the story through the days of the week.
- Notice that both Mum and Dad look after Tom.

Reading the text
- Ensure the children read the days of the week written in italics at the top of the page.
- Encourage the children to read the direct speech in the way the characters would say it.
- If 'stay' is a difficult word on page 4, compare it with 'day' and change the first letters.

Revisiting the text
- Get the children to retell the story in their own words using the days of the week as a starting point, for example:
  On Monday Tom felt ill.
  On Tuesday he woke up with a fat face.
- Discuss the times when the children have felt ill and who looked after them.
- Read the following list of words and ask the children to identify when they hear a word with a long 'e' sound as in 'sleep': bed, sleep, egg, speak, when, Ben, read, said, clean, went, fed, keep.
- Play tic-tac-toe with the group. Write a regular verb and ask the children to write the past tense, as follows:

look		stayed
	looked	
	stay	

Writing activities
- The children could write a get-well card for Tom.
- As a shared or guided activity, write a letter to Tom or to a child who is absent. A writing frame, similar to the one below, would provide a useful scaffold for supporting writing:
  Dear _____ .
  At school today we _____ .
- Ask the children to make a group book describing various illnesses:
  Mumps
  You get a fat face.
  Chickenpox
  You get spots that itch.
  A cold
  You get a runny nose and a sore throat.
- Alternatively, they could make a diary chart for a week in school, such as this:
  On Monday
  We went to singing
  On Tuesday
  It rained and we had wet play.

Poems, rhymes and jingles
Mumps
I had a feeling in my neck
And on the sides
Were two big lumps
I couldn't swallow
Anything at all
Because I had the mumps.

Elizabeth Madox Roberts

Word level work	Sentence level work	Text level work	High-frequency words
To extend the child's vocabulary by learning and reading the days of the week.	To read direct speech in the way the characters would say it.	To re-tell the story, and to understand the sequence of the story through the days of the week.	on, came, home, after, school, and, said, not, going, to, bed, Mum, come, here, in, bed, we, will, look, you, like, this, he, went, to, is, for, at, my, going, down, where, are, they, away

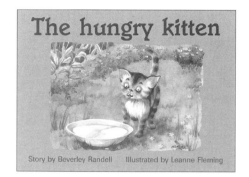

The hungry kitten
Story by Beverley Randell
Illustrations by Leanne Fleming

Level: Yellow Set 1
Genre: Story with predictable language
Running words: 88
Links to other PM titles: *A home for Little Teddy; A friend for little white rabbit; Little Bulldozer* (Thematic)

Overview
The hungry kitten follows a similar format and structure to *A home for Little Teddy*, in which the main character tries to find a place where he is accepted. The dialogue makes it suitable for role-playing to highlight the different characters and expression needed to convey the story.

Introducing the text
- Read the title and discuss the reasons why the little kitten might be hungry.
- On page 3, predict whether the hungry little kitten will drink the milk. Ensure the children hear and locate the word 'Miaow'.
- On pages 8 and 9, ensure the children understand the dog is growling and locate the letters representing the sound.
- On page 8, predict what will happen to the hungry little kitten.
- On page 13, discuss whether the boy will feed the hungry little kitten.

Reading the text
- 'Little' is not part of the title. Observe whether the children notice 'little' on page 2.
- Look at page 12. Use picture cues and questions related to what you say when you meet someone to prompt 'Hello'. Ensure the children cross-check with the letter cues.
- Encourage the children to use the tension in the story to read expressively.

Revisiting the text
- Return to the illustrations to describe how the little kitten was feeling. Discuss how the children felt at various points in the story, for example after the kitten had been chased away by the big dog.
- Use one of the illustrations of the little kitten and ask the children to describe it. Encourage the children to give more than one-word descriptions.
- Make a word string of words ending with 'nt', such as: 'went', 'bent', 'want', 'meant', 'pint', 'tent'.
- Make a list of sounds represented by letters, for example: Grrrr , sh-sh-sh, choo-choo-choo, wooooo, mmmm.
Help the children to say the sounds with expression.

Writing activities
- Help the children to write instructions on how to look after a pet by offering structured sentences such as:
    I give my _____ (milk).
    I give my _____ (a basket to sleep in).
- Ask the children to write a chart about what a kitten would need. Provide prompts such as:
    A kitten will need:
    – food
    – a home
    – milk
- Children might like to write about their own or friends' pets to make a wall story. Encourage them to use descriptive words.
- Using the illustrations on pages 11 to 13 allow the children to write thought bubbles for the kitten.

Poems, rhymes and jingles

> **Little grey kitten**
> A little grey kitten
> with big yellow eyes
> Looked in a mirror
> with the greatest surprise
> For there in the mirror
> and just the same size
> Was a little grey kitten
> with big yellow eyes.
> *Zheyna Gay*

Word level work	Sentence level work	Text level work	High-frequency words
To look at lists of sounds represented by letters, for example 'Grrr', 'sh-sh', 'Choo-choo'.	To use the tension in the story to read with expression.	To use a range of phonological, contextual, grammatical and graphic cues to work out, predict and check meanings of words within the text.	I, like, this, said, a, little, go, away, big, cat, dog, went, boy, are, you, we, will, look, after, the, here

Sally's beans

Story by Beverley Randell
Illustrations by Meredith Thomas

Level: Yellow Set 1
Genre: Story with familiar language
Running words: 123
Links to other PM titles: *Sally and the daisy; Sally and the sparrows; Sally's red bucket*

Overview
Re-read *Sally and the daisy* and try to establish the kind of setting in which the stories about Sally and her mum take place. What does Sally enjoy doing? What can be deduced from the illustrations? Alternatively, this text could be used in conjuction with non-fiction texts about plants, leading on to discussions based on personal experiences. You may wish to accumulate different text types about growing things in order to build up fact files.

Introducing the text
- Read the title and discuss what the story is going to be about. Discuss any experiences the children may have had of growing things.
- Make sure the children understand what Sally is doing on page 6.
- Look at page 9. Discuss why only seven beans have come up. Predict what has happened to the others.
- Use the illustration on page 10 to help the children predict 'watered'.
- Make sure the children realise what Mum is looking at on page 12.

Reading the text
- If 'garden' is a difficult word, ask the children to sound the 'ar' part of the word (relating it to 'car' if necessary), and then add in the 'g'. Refer back to the meaning by asking the child to re-read 'Mum went into the gar...'
- Observe whether the children notice the bold text to help them read with expression.
- Observe whether the children use the illustration and letter cues to read 'watered' on page 10.

Revisiting the text
- Revisit the text to make a list of the things the beans needed to grow.

- Make a list of other vegetables Sally could grow in her garden. Discuss which vegetables the children like.
- Play a version of 'hangman' using words from the story. (See page 55 for instructions.)
- Play tic-tac-toe with words beginning with 'th'. Use two different coloured pens, one for the teacher's words, and one for the children's words. The children could find 'th' words in the story to help them.

the	those	them
they	thing	thin
this	that	there

Writing activities
- Help the children to write a list of instructions for planting beans by providing the first steps:
    1. Dig a small hole.
    2. Put a bean in the hole.
- In a shared writing activity, make a wall display of vegetables. The children then write captions about their likes or dislikes.
- Help the children to write a 'bean' poem using a known format:

    _____ beans _____ beans
    _____ beans _____ beans
    Last of all
    Best of all
    I like _____ beans.

- Get the children to write two or three adjectives to describe known vegetables:
    A little round green pea.
    A round red juicy tomato.

Poems, rhymes and jingles
A spike of green

When I went out
The sun was hot
It shone upon
My flower pot.

And there I saw
A spike of green
That no one else
Had ever seen!

On other days
The things I see
Are mostly old
Except for me.

But this green spike
So new and small
Had never yet
Been seen at all.

Barbara Baker

Word level work	Sentence level work	Text level work	High-frequency words
To read on sight the high-frequency words specific to the book.	To notice the bold text to help read with expression.	To discuss Sally as a character. From this story and the other story what does Sally enjoy doing? What is Sally doing to the plants in this story?	Mum, went, the, too, here, you, are, said, for, in, day, after, come, up, where, my, look, ten, water, they, and, down, this, see, little, green, big, look, at, I, like

Baby Hippo

Story by Beverley Randell
Illustrations by Elizabeth Russell-Arnot

Level: Yellow Set 1
Genre: Story with predictable structure
Running words: 118
Links to other PM titles: *Tiger, Tiger; Blackberries; Brave Father Mouse; Mumps* (Thematic)

Overview

This story has a parallel theme to *Tiger, Tiger*. It may be useful for children to compare and contrast the differences. Encourage them to start using words such as 'setting' and 'characters'. There are also thematic similarities with the sense of parental protection explored in *Blackberries*, *Mumps* and *Tiger, Tiger*. You may wish your children to start organising the information they've gleaned from the Storybooks (and elsewhere) about how good parents look after their children.

Introducing the text

- Read the title and find Baby Hippo. Tell the children that 'hippo' is short for 'hippopotamus'. Discuss where the hippos live and what other animals live in the same areas.
- Look at page 4. Remind the children about the story *Tiger, Tiger* (Red Set). Predict whether Baby Hippo will wake up like Baby Monkey did.
- Look at pages 8 and 9. Check the children's predictions and predict which animal is going to hunt Baby Hippo.
- Look at page 11. Predict whether Baby Hippo will see the lions. Will he be safe?
- Confirm the predictions on pages 13 and 16.

Reading the text

- Observe whether the children read all the plurals in the text.
- If a child reads 'water' for 'river' on page 4 agree that this makes sense, but ask him/her to reread the sentence focusing on the first letter of 'river'. Observe whether the child is using both picture and letter cues on pages 8 and 9.
- Encourage the children to read pages 13 to 15 with a sense of drama.

Revisiting the text

- Discuss why Baby Hippo and Baby Monkey should not have gone for a walk by themselves. How did Mother Hippo react differently from Mother Monkey?
- Ask whether the children have visited the zoo and seen hippos. Discuss what they know about hippos.
- Make headbands or finger-puppets and put on a play of Baby Hippo.
- Reinforce the 'y' sound at the end of Baby. Make a list of words ending in 'y' that make the same sound.
- Make 'asleep' with magnetic letters. Find 'a' and 'sleep'. Ask the children to find another similar word on page 14.

Writing activities

- Using the text, ask the children to write some facts about hippos, such as:
    Hippos are bigger than lions.
    They lie in the water.
    Baby hippos sleep on their mother's backs in the water.
- Get the children to write about how the children's parents/carers keep them safe, for example:
    Mum comes with me to the park.
    Dad goes in the water with me.
- Draw a large hippo for the wall. Get the children to write descriptive phrases.

Poems, rhymes and jingles

My hippo

I'm trying to draw a hippo,
The way to start, I know,
Is with a great big oval –

And then I'll make him grow.
Two circles for his head, with ears,
And eyes and mouth and nose,

And when I've done his tail and legs
I'll give him lots of toes.

Beverley Randell

Word level work	Sentence level work	Text level work	High Frequency words
To look at the plurals in the text, focusing on those ending with 's'.	To predict words from preceding words in sentences to make sense of text.	To choose and read other books on a similar theme about parental protection. To discuss preferences and give reasons.	the, are, down, in, can, you, see, is, too, he, on, they, like, going, and, for, a, up, not, at, here, come, she, big, away, back

Jolly Roger, the pirate

Story by Beverley Randell
Illustrations by Chantal Stewart

Level: Yellow Set 1
Genre: Story with predictable structure
Running words: 132
Links to other PM titles: *Ben's Teddy Bear; Ben's Treasure Hunt* (Thematic)

Overview
As in *Ben's Teddy Bear* and *Ben's Treasure Hunt*, readers are given picture cues that give them access to information that the characters don't have. You may wish to draw attention to the presentation of some of the dialogue in speech bubbles by talking about the different ways of presenting direct speech.

Introducing the text
- Read the title and notice what items of clothing Jolly Roger has taken off. Notice what he is still wearing.
- Look at pages 2 and 3 and discuss why the pirates are hiding Jolly Roger's clothes. Predict where they will hide them.
- Discuss what Jolly Roger is looking for on page 10.
- Read page 13 with the children. Discuss why the pirates are telling Jolly Roger to look in the sea. Predict what will happen next.

Reading the text
- Encourage the children to read the text in direct speech as if it were being spoken.
- Observe whether the children use initial letter cues to read 'coat' and 'boot' accurately.
- Observe whether the children read both the words 'big' and 'boots'. Ask them to re-read if 'big' is omitted.

Revisiting the text
- Ask the children how this book is similar to *Ben's treasure hunt* and *Ben's Teddy Bear*.

- Ensure the children are able to explain how the pirate's hat ended up in the sea.
- Discuss why the pirates played tricks on Jolly Roger. Discuss any tricks the children have played.
- Find all the words in the text with a long 'e' sound. Read parts of the text to the children. Ask them to put up their hands, or clap, when they hear a long 'e' sound on pages 8 and 12.
- Segment and blend 'hat'. Ask the children to write all the letters. Write 'hat' with magnetic letters and change the medial vowel to create words such as: hat, hit, hut, hot.

Writing activities
- Ask the children to imagine what would happened if the pirates had turned hunting the clothes into a treasure hunt. Then get them to write the clues that the pirates would have needed.
- Ask them to describe where the pirates were going in their ship.
- The children could write a letter to Jolly Roger, telling him how he could avoid having his clothes stolen from him in the future.

Poems, rhymes and jingles

The pirate
Once there was a pirate
as wicked as can be.
He sailed on his pirate ship
across the deep blue sea.
He had a wooden leg
and a patch across one eye.
And a parrot on his shoulder
who couldn't even fly!
He had a crew of mates
raggedy and strong.
And once they found the treasure
They all went sailing home.

Word level work	Sentence level work	Text level work	High-frequency words
To look at all the words in the text with a long 'e' sound.	To read the speech 'like talking' and to notice how direct speech is shown here by the speech bubbles.	To re-tell the story, giving the main points in sequence, and to notice the difference between written and spoken forms in re-telling.	is, said, the, we, will, his, up, where, are, my, big, he, here, they, I, can, see, went, to, look, for, not, in, up, down

Lucky goes to dog school

Story by Beverley Randell
Illustrations by Warren Crossett

Level: Yellow Set 2
Genre: Story with predictable structure
Running words: 127
Links to other PM titles: *Choosing a puppy; Tiny and the big wave* (Thematic)

Overview
Lucky goes to dog school is a simple narrative in which the different elements of the story are easy to identify and compare. Ensure that children are aware of the difference between Lucky's behaviour at the beginning of the story and at the end of the story. How does this affect Dad and Rachel's feelings about Lucky? What happens in the middle of the story to make the ending possible?

Introducing the text
- Read the title and the notice on the front cover. Discuss what a dog school could be and why Lucky would need to go.
- Ensure the children know the names of the characters.
- Discuss why Dad and Rachel are cross with Lucky on pages 2 to 5.
- On page 7, confirm predictions from the initial discussion.
- Predict whether Lucky will learn to be obedient. Confirm predictions on pages 15 and 16.

Reading the text
- Encourage the children to use letter cues to work out 'woof'.
- Encourage the children to cross-check meaning with letter cues on page 5, if 'naughty' is a difficult word to read.
- Encourage the children to use the character's frustration with Lucky to read expressively.

Revisiting the text
- Draw on the children's own experiences of pets being disobedient. Discuss the feelings of the owners involved and compare these with how Dad and Rachel felt.

- Contrast Rachel and Dad's feelings at the beginning of the story to those at the end.
- Find words in the text with 'oo' such as 'woof' and 'school'. Decide if the words all make the same sound in the middle.
- Revise the words ending with 'y' and add to the list of words found in previous stories.
- Make a string of words ending with the same phoneme as 'sit'. Change the initial consonant and medial vowel to make new words, for example:
sit sat bit bat cat cut

Writing activities
- Draw a large dog for the wall. Get the children to write statements about dogs, for example:
   Some dogs have long ears.
   Dogs wag their tails.
- Help the children to write a recount about a pet being disobedient by providing a writing plan like this:

When	Where	What

- The children could rewrite the story in their own words, putting the story into sequence.
   Lucky ran out into the road.
   Rachel and Dad couldn't catch him.
   Dad saw the notice for the dog school.

Speaking and listening
- Owning a pet is a responsibility. Discuss the things that a responsible dog owner needs to do. Ask pupils to sketch a role-play in which one is Rachel asking Dad for a puppy. What would Dad say?

Poems. rhymes and jingles
Dogs
The dogs I know have many shapes
For some are big and tall
And some are long and some are thin
And some are fat and small
And some are little bits of fluff
And have no shape at all.
Marchette Chute

Word level work	Sentence level work	Text level work	High-frequency words
To use final and medial letter sounds in simple words taken from the text, for example words ending with 'y', and changing medial vowels to make new words.	To use the character's frustration with Lucky to read with expression.	To compare Lucky's behaviour at the beginning of the story and at the end. What happens in the middle to make the ending possible?	Dad, and, went, to, the, a, is, said, come, here, dog, look, at, this, school, in, no, came, help, like, he, with, me, down, home, good

Ben's dad

Story by Beverley Randell
Illustrations by Genevieve Rees

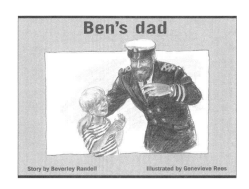

Level: Yellow Set 2
Genre: Story with predictable structure
Running words: 103
Links to other PM titles: *Ben's Teddy Bear; Ben's treasure hunt; A birthday cake for Ben*

Overview
The fifth book in the Ben series reveals the reason why we seldom see Ben's dad. He works on board a ship and is consequently away from home much of the time. Ensure that the children understand Ben's excitement at his father's return, and are able to list all the events that show Ben's excitement.

Introducing the text
- Show the children the book *Ben's Teddy Bear* and the picture Ben had beside his bed. Then show them the new book *Ben's dad* and discuss what work Ben's dad does.
- Discuss why Ben is so excited on page 2.
- Ensure the children know where Ben is on page 4, and who he is talking to.
- Discuss Ben's picture on pages 8 and 9 and what Ben's father does on the ship.
- Predict who will come to collect Ben from school.

Reading the text
- If a child reads 'said' for 'shouted' on page 3, encourage self-correction by saying 'You made a mistake on that page. Read it again and look carefully at the words'.
- Observe whether the children are using picture and letter cues on page 7.
- Observe how the children attempt to read 'engines' on page 11. Encourage them to use letter cues and the picture on pages 8 and 9.
- Use picture cues to work out what time of the day it is on page 13.

Revisiting the text
- Play 'Who Am I?' with the children by giving them clues, for example: 'I wear a black hat. I drive a big red truck with a siren. Who am I?'
- Make a list of words to describe how Ben was feeling in the story. Extend the children's vocabulary by introducing words they may not have come up with such as 'excited'.
- Discuss what a 'uniform' is and name occupations where people have to wear one.
- Make a game for the group in which they match cards onto a base board. The base board has the names of different occupations, for example: teacher, fireman, policeman, nurse. The cards have a statement about the job, for example, 'I put out fires'.
- Make a word wheel for words ending with 'ip'. Encourage children to think of two phonemes at the beginning, for example: flip, trip, clip.

Writing activities
- The children could write statements about people's occupations. Some of these statements could be correct, and others not, for example:
    A builder uses a hammer.
    A fireman gives people medicine.
- Allow children to read each other's statements and stick them under 'yes' or 'no' headings using blu-tack.
- Let the children write about times when they are happy and sad.
- Allow them to write about what they would like to do when they grow up.
- The children could prepare a question or questions to ask the school secretary or caretaker about his or her job. An opportunity should be found for the group to ask their questions and write or record the answer.

Poems, rhymes and jingles
This happy day
Every morning when the sun
Comes smiling up on everyone
It's lots of fun
To say good morning to the sun
Good morning sun

Every evening after play
When the sunshine goes away
It's nice to say
Thank you for this happy day
This happy day.
Harry Behn

Word level work	Sentence level work	Text level work	High-frequency words
To extend vocabulary by listing words to describe how Ben was feeling in the story.	To introduce new punctuation mark: the dash.	To use letter and picture cues to predict and check meanings of unfamiliar words, and to make sense of what the children read.	Mum, said, Dad, is, home, went, to, school, my, he, the, going, where, your, look, with, down, here, at, after, on, and

The new baby

Story by Beverley Randell
Illustrations by Ernest Papps

Level: Yellow Set 2
Genre: Story with familiar language
Running words: 130
Links to other PM titles: *The big kick; Sausages; Tom is brave; Mumps;*

Overview

Compare this account of the arrival of Tom's baby sister, Emma, with the non-fiction book *Our Baby*. Ensure that your pupils notice the difference in type of illustrations (pictures versus photographs), layout, presentation of information and narrative structure. Note the similarities too. As well as introducing a new baby into Tom's family, this story also involves Tom's grandparents, Poppa and Nana. The role of grandparents in the family is explored in the non-fiction book *My Gran and Grandad*.

Introducing the text

- Discuss the children's experiences of having a new baby in the house.
- Ensure the children know the names of the characters in the story.
- On page 5 discuss why Mum is not home and why Poppa is there.
- Look at page 9 and discuss why Poppa is asleep in a chair.
- Ensure the children understand that Tom and Poppa go to the hospital the next day.

Reading the text

- On page 4 there is an explanation of why Mum is not at home. The children cannot use the illustrations for cues. Observe the strategies they use instead, for example, re-running for meaning, and use of letter cues.
- Observe any cross-checking between picture and letter cues on page 6.
- Observe the children's use of letter cues on page 10.

Revisiting the text

- Talk about how Tom might be feeling on pages 2 to 9 with Mum and Dad not in the house.
- Look at page 13 and make a list of words to describe how Tom and Poppa are feeling.
- Discuss ways in which Tom could help with Emma.
- Reinforce 'ed' and 'ing' endings. Ask the children to find examples in the text. Get them to spell the base word.
- Reinforce the long 'e' sound. Find an example in the text and make a list of other words.

Writing activities

- Write a list of the things Tom could do to help his mother with the new baby.
- Ask the children to pretend they are Tom in order to write a letter to a friend telling them about Emma.
- Ask the children to look at the illustration of Poppa and write a description of a grandparent.
- Draw a picture of a baby for the wall and get the children to write captions about babies.

Word level work	Sentence level work	Text level work	High-frequency words
To read on sight 30 more high-frequency words to aid reading.	To use awareness of the grammar of a sentence to decipher new or unfamiliar words.	To compare/contrast the styles of a 'fiction' and 'non-fiction' book. Take note of type of illustrations, layout, presentation of information and narrative structure.	came, home, after, school, he, said, where, is, Mum, at, the, Dad, with, too, I, am, here, you, will, help, like, went, to, bed, up, a, girl, see, going, look, little

Baby Bear goes fishing

Story by Beverley Randell
Illustrations by Isabel Lowe

Level: Yellow Set 2
Genre: Story with elements of fantasy
Running words: 112
Links to other PM titles: *Father Bear goes fishing; Blackberries*

Overview
Both Father Bear and Mother Bear think that Baby Bear is too little to go fishing, but Baby Bear surprises them both by catching a full net of fish for supper. Contrast the setting of this Bear story with earlier titles, and deduce what this tells us about the Bear family. See whether children can empathise with Baby Bear's triumph at proving his parents wrong, and whether they've ever felt that way.

Introducing the text
- Read the title and remind the children about the story *Father Bear goes fishing*. Discuss reasons why Father Bear goes fishing.
- Look at page 4 and discuss why Mother Bear is looking anxious.
- Ensure the children hear and use the word 'river' on page 7.
- On page 9 predict what is going to happen and who is going to be successful at fishing.

Reading the text
- Note that the story begins with Father Bear talking. Encourage the children to begin reading 'in character'.
- Look at page 3. Children often confuse 'help' with 'play'. Encourage self-correction by asking the child to re-read the sentence to make sense.
- Observe whether the children notice 'shouted' on page 13 where 'said' has been used on all other pages.
- Observe whether the children use the bold text and punctation as an aid for expressive reading.

Revisiting the text
- Discuss the activities families do together in their leisure time. Some children may have had experiences of going fishing.
- Revisit the illustrations on pages 8 to 11. Contrast how Father Bear and Baby Bear are feeling. Encourage the children to elaborate on why they think they are feeling that way.
- Revise the use of capital letters. For example, notice how Father Bear is written with initial capitals, as is 'Fish' on page 13.
- Revise 'too' at the end of Baby Bear's speech on page 3 and on page 5.
- Practise hearing and writing the sounds in CVC words like 'not' and 'big', and words with three phonemes like 'with' and 'fish'.
- Revise compound words and see whether children can spot one in the story. (For example, 'today' on page 8.)

Writing activities
- Ask the children to write captions for a wall story or book about bear/fish facts that the children know, for example:
  Fish swim in rivers.
  Bears like to eat fish.
- Ask the children to write speech bubbles for the illustrations on pages 10 or 14.
- Tell them to make a list of the things they would need if they were to go fishing.
- They could write a recount of a family activity, for example:
  I go to the football with my dad.
  I go to visit my Gran on Sundays with my mum and dad.

Poems, rhymes and jingles
Fish
The little fish are silent
As they swim round and round
Their mouths are ever talking
A speech without a sound.

Arthur S. Bourinot

Word level work	Sentence level work	Text level work	High-frequency words
To reinforce regular ending to present tense words: -ing; going; fishing; coming.	To self-correct by asking the children to re-read to make the sentence make sense.	To re-read the story and look at significant incidents in the story. Contrast this with *Father Bear goes fishing*.	going, said, I, like, too, will, go, with, you, and, help, are, little, to, am, not, big, went, down, the, come, here, on, look, at, my, home

Hermit Crab

Story by Beverley Randell
Illustrations by Julian Bruere

Level: Yellow Set 2
Genre: Story with predictable structure
Running words: 114
Links to other PM titles: *Lizard loses his tail; Brave Father Mouse; Baby Hippo; A lucky day for Little Dinosaur* (Thematic)

Overview

Another story about a smaller animal that manages to avoid becoming a meal for a larger one, *Hermit Crab* provides another story to compare and contrast with titles that have similar themes. Unlike previous stories, this is told in a combination of narrated prose and rhyme. Use this text to consolidate the use of different typefaces to reinforce meaning. Look at the problem set out on page 2, and how the problem is resolved on the last page. Think of alternative endings to the story.

Introducing the text

- Explore the children's knowledge of crabs. Ensure the children understand how a hermit crab is different from an ordinary crab.
- On page 3 ensure the children realise that the shell is the crab's home, but she has grown too big for it.
- Build the tension of the story line by asking questions about what will happen to Hermit Crab.
- Draw the children's attention to why the words are written in italics on page 14. (The story becomes a rhyme here.)
- Ensure the children hear and use the word 'safe' on page 16.

Reading the text

- Observe whether the children distinguish between 'she' on page 2 and 'he' on page 8.
- Observe whether the children use their knowledge of compound words to work out 'inside' on page 2.
- Observe whether the children notice the tension in the story as they read.

Revisiting the text

- Re-read page 14 together, and enjoy the rhythmical pattern.

- Plot the story together for problems and how the hermit crab tried to solve them, for example:

1st problem	the shell was too little.
Solution	find another shell.
2nd problem	the shell was occupied.
Solution	find another shell.
3rd problem..........	

- Ask the children to hear the sounds in 'crab' and spell the word. Try other words like 'crash' and 'creep'.
- Practise hearing final phonemes of words like 'shell' and 'fish'. Use pictures or objects in a bag for children to choose and say the name. Use a glove puppet which mispronounces the word for the children to correct, for example, for 'shell' the puppet would say 'shed'. As an extension, ask the children to give the letter/s of the final phoneme.

Writing activities

- Get the children to write a 'Who am I?' quiz for a friend to read. For example,
  Who am I?
  I live in the sea.
  I eat crabs.
- Let the children make a book with illustrations, about homes for animals, such as:
  This is a home for a dog.
  This is a home for a bird.
- Discuss the features of a crab. Give the children a picture of a crab to label, and provide labels for parts such as: 'pincers', 'legs', 'eyes', 'feelers'.

Poems, rhymes and jingles

My shell
When I went down to the sea today
I found a shell and it seemed to say
sh…sh…sh…
And as I listened it seemed to me
There was someone inside. Now who could it be?
sh…sh…sh
But it wasn't a fish or a mermaid
It was just the lovely sound of the sea
Forever caught in my shell for me
Sh…sh… sh…

Word level work	Sentence level work	Text level work	High-frequency words
To look at initial consonant clusters related to the story, for example 'cr' – crab, creep, crash.	To draw attention to the reason why some words are written in italics.	To be aware that story is a combination of narrated prose and rhyme. Learn the simple rhyme and re-read it from the text.	at, home, she, is, a, too, big, for, this, little, here, will, look, no, to, help, where, good, going, away, not, you

Sally and the sparrows

Story by Jenny Giles
Illustrations by Meredith Thomas

Level: Yellow Set 2
Genre: Story with predictable structure
Running words: 151
Links to other PM titles: *Sally and the daisy; Sally's beans; Sally's red bucket*

Overview

This story reinforces the reader's perception about Sally as a nature-loving person. Is there anything that children can add to their character profile about Sally? Look at the artwork to see how the layout and design compare with previous Sally titles. Are all the stories illustrated by the same person? This title also provides plenty of material for phonic level work, for instance the long 'ee' sound, the phoneme blend 'st', 'sp', and the final phoneme 'y'.

Introducing the text

- Remind the children about *Pussy and the birds* and the noises the birds made. Discuss why Sally is looking at the birds on the front cover. Ensure the children use the word 'sparrows'.
- Discuss the time of day on page 2, and how the sparrows are feeling in the morning.
- Look at page 4. Note how Sally is dressed and why she is not going to stay in bed.
- Predict how Sally will get the birds to come down on page 8.
- Confirm predictions on pages 15 and 16.

Reading the text

- If 'stay' is a difficult word on page 5, make 'day' and a short rhyming string to 'stay'.
- If a child substitutes 'grass' for 'garden' on page 7, confirm that the attempt was almost right and direct the child to the final sounds.
- If 'inside' on page 11 is a difficult word, direct the child to picture cues and 'in'.
- Allow self-correction by encouraging the children to re-read and use picture cues on pages 13 to 16.

Revisiting the text

- Return to the illustration on page 4. Discuss Sally's actions. Ask the children to describe times when they have been the first to wake up.
- Discuss what Sally's problem was in the story (she wanted the birds to come down) and how she solved it. Could she have found another solution?
- Read 'stay' to the children. Ask them to look on page 15 for another word in the story that starts the same way. Read the following list to the children, and ask them to respond with 'yes' or 'no' depending on whether the word starts with the same letters as 'stay': story, start, sparrow, stop, spin.
- Read parts of the story to the children. Ask them to listen for the long 'e' sound, for example on pages 7 and 9. Contrast this with the short 'e' sound on page 11.

Writing activities

- Ask the children to write the story in their own words. They should first plan first using words like first, next, at the end.
- The children could write a recount of their own experiences on waking up on a Saturday or Sunday, for example:
    I wake up and watch TV.
    I wake up and play with my Lego.
- Return to the illustration on the title page which shows a male (left) and a female sparrow (right). Provide a chart for the children to write the differences.

Poems, rhymes and jingles

A little bird's song

Sometimes I've seen,	Sometimes he stays,
Sometimes I've heard,	Sometimes he sings,
Up in a tree,	Then to the wind,
A little bird,	He spreads his wings,
Singing a song,	Flying away,
A song to me,	Away from me,
A little brown bird,	A little brown bird,
Up in a tree.	Up in a tree.

Word level work	Sentence level work	Text level work	High-frequency words
To look at words with the long 'ee' sound. To read parts of the story to hear the sound.	To expect reading to make sense and check if it does not through a variety of cues.	To re-tell the story, including the sequence of events and highlighting significant events, for example what Sally's problem was and how she solved it.	the, came, up, and, said, too, not, to, in, bed, she, go, see, going, went, I, can, you, tree, come, down, me, at, they, are, get, some, for, like, ran, here, is, on, with, little, came

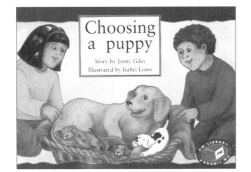

Choosing a puppy

Story by Jenny Giles
Illustrations by Isabel Lowe

Level: Yellow Set 2
Genre: Story with predictable structure
Running words: 158
Links to other PM titles: *The little snowman;*

Overview
Remind your pupils of their previous encounter with Rachel and Sam. This story is told from the children's perspective. You may wish your pupils to retell the story as if they were the puppy meeting Sam and Rachel for the first time. Make sure that they use established narrative conventions to tell the story. Consider the role played by a pet in family life.

Introducing the text
- Discuss which puppy the children themselves would choose. Ask the children for their reasons.
- Look at pages 6 and 7, and predict which puppy the children will choose.
- Look at page 10 and discuss whether Rachel will change her mind.

Reading the text
- Observe whether the children notice the plural 'puppies'.
- The children could work out Andy's name by finding 'And' and adding a 'y' sound.
- Observe whether the children use initial letters to distinguish the characters' names.
- Direct the children to picture cues on page 6 if 'brown' is a difficult word.

Revisiting the text
- Look at the illustration on page 13. Discuss the book Andy is giving Dad, what it is about, and why Dad would need it.

- Think of some alliterative names for the puppies, for example Peter puppy or Daniel dog.
- Revise words ending with 'y' and add puppy and Andy to the existing list.
- Look at 'Spot got' on page 12 and make a rhyming string.

Writing activities
- Ask each child to write a page for the *How to care for your puppy* manual, for example:
    Give your puppy a ... (bed, toy, water, bone, bath).
- Ask the children to write about the pets that they have at home.
- Ask them to decide which puppy they would choose and write why, for example:
    I like the brown puppy because...
- Get them to write a simple advertisement to sell the puppies, using one adjective. Discuss words that describe puppies, for example:
    mischievous, playful, fat, sleepy.
Provide the children with the words on cards.

Poems, rhymes and jingles
Pets
Whether your pet
is a dog or a cat,
a horse or a bird
or a mouse or a rat.
It gives love and friendship
in its own way to you,
and it needs you to feed it
and care for it too.

Word level work	Sentence level work	Text level work	High-frequency words
To make a new word list of words ending with 'y', for example Andy and puppy.	To be aware of capital letters as cues to distinguish characters' names.	To identify and use established narrative conventions to re-tell the story from the dog's perspective.	said, come, and, see, the, they, are, here, in, with, dog, look, Dad, can, a, you, like, I, this, little, brown, is, went, for, on, down, up, at, look, he, me, to, got, we, home, us

Football at the park

Story by Jenny Giles
Illustrations by Trish Hill

Level: Yellow Set 2
Genre: Story with predictable structure
Running words: 131
Links to other PM titles: None

Overview

This is the first of the stories about Tim. Unlike the mini-series featuring other families, these take place away from Tim's home. You may wish to elaborate on the story's theme of exclusion by linking the story to issues covered in citizenship or PSHE. Ask pupils to list all the excuses that other children give for not playing with newcomers. See whether they can make a connection between this story and *Baby Bear goes fishing*, in which Baby Bear's family thinks he is too small to do something.

Introducing the text

- Read the title and discuss what the story is going to be about.
- Page 2 introduces Tim. Predict whether the big boys will let Tim play on page 4. Confirm the prediction on page 6.
- Predict what will happen on pages 8 and 9.
- Confirm predictions on pages 10 to 13, and predict the end of the story. Confirm the prediction on pages 14 to 16.

Reading the text

- Encourage the children to notice the speech marks and to read 'like talking'.
- Observe whether the children notice the repeated phrase 'all the way' on pages 10 and 13. If 'all' is a difficult word, compare with 'ball'.
- Observe whether the children use the picture cues on page 8 to help them read.
- Observe whether the children notice the 'a' in 'came'.

Revisiting the text

- Look at the illustrations on pages 7 to 9. Ask the children to describe how Tim was feeling. Contrast this with how he felt on pages 15 and 16. Ask the children to expand on why Tim was feeling that way.
- Discuss the children's experience of being included or excluded from older children's games and how they felt.
- Make rhyming strings with 'all'.
- Revise compound words such as 'into', 'inside', and 'away' from previous books.
- Ask the children to find another example, such as 'football'.

Writing activities

- Ask children to choose either page 7 or page 15 and write about Tim, using one of the feeling words discussed earlier:
    Tim was … when he …
- Make a wall story about the children's favourite games. Ask the children a page about themselves.
    Andrew likes to play football.
    Amerjit likes to …
- Ask the children to write a 'happy-sad' book:
    I am happy when …
    I am sad when …

Poems, rhymes and jingles

Playing football
We're running up and down the field,
Trying to get the ball…
The other team is winning…
We have no points at all.

But here we come! It's our turn now!
The crowd begins to roar!
We're heading down towards the goal…
And this time we will score!

Jenny Giles

Word level work	Sentence level work	Text level work	High-frequency words
To look at common spelling patterns, for example all/ball.	To be aware of the speech marks and to read 'like talking'.	To use a wide range of cues to work out, predict and check what has been read to ensure that the text makes sense.	at, the, they, ball, up, and, down, said, can, I, play, with, you, like, no, a, boy, are, too, little, to, us, went, away, back, big, ran, it, came, all, down, way, come, on, good, for

Seagull is clever

Story by Beverley Randell
Illustrations by Ernest Papps

Level: Yellow Set 3
Genre: Story with predictable language
Running words: 98
Links to other PM titles: *Hermit Crab; Tiger, Tiger; Tall Things; Sally and the sparrows; A lucky day for Little Dinosaur* (Thematic)

Overview

Although this title belongs within the Storybooks genre range, it contains a combination of factual and subjective information. Although there is a narrative which links the presentation of facts, it is formulated within the context of the types of questions children should be asking themselves when reading expository text types. 'Will Seagull get a fish?'; 'Where is Seagull going?'; 'Is Seagull eating the shellfish?'. This book may be used as an information text as children may find it more accessible than some expository-type information texts.

Introducing the text

- Read the title and discuss the concept of 'clever'. Discuss ways in which a seagull could be clever.
- Look at page 4 and discuss why Seagull cannot find a fish today.
- Ensure the children use the word 'shellfish' on page 7 and understand what a shellfish is.
- Predict what will happen when Seagull drops the shellfish on page 13.
- Confirm predictions on page 15 by looking at the broken shellfish. Ensure the children use the word 'broken'.
- Confirm how Seagull was clever on page 16.

Reading the text

- If children mis-read 'waves' on page 5 (substituting 'water' or 'sea'), encourage self-correction by asking them to re-read, looking carefully at the initial and middle letters.
- Encourage the children to use letter knowledge and knowledge of compound words to read 'shellfish'.
- Encourage the use of picture cues on pages 11 and 13.
- If 'bird' is a difficult word on page 16 give children three choices to check against the word, for example:
    He is a clever seagull/animal/bird.
  If the child chooses 'bird', ask him/her how they knew that was right.

Revisiting the text

- Plot the story together for problems and how Seagull solved them:
    1st problem   the waves were too big.
    Solution   find a shellfish.
    2nd problem...
- Ask the children to name some birds. Remind them about *Sally and the sparrows*. Write a chart of characteristics all birds have in common, for example:
    All birds have: wings
                     two feet
                     a beak
- Revise compound words and add 'seagull' and 'shellfish'.
- Revise adding 'ing' and 's' to words. Find 'goes' in the text and discover what is different.
- Read pages 5 and 16 to the children and ask them to identify words with 'v' in the middle, for example: 'waves' or 'clever'.
- Extend the children's vocabulary by asking them to give alternative words for 'broken' and 'clever'.

Writing activities

- Discuss a problem the children have had and how they solved it, then get them to write a page for a 'clever' book.
- Give the children a picture of a bird for them to label, for example: wings, beak.
- Write a different solution for Seagull's problem of being hungry.
- Write a 'bird' poem using a known format:
    _____ birds _____ birds
    _____ birds _____ birds
    Last of all
    Best of all
    I like _____ birds.

Word level work	Sentence level work	Text level work	High-frequency words
To recognise words by common spelling patterns, for example, looking at compound words such as 'shellfish' and 'seagull'.	If a word is difficult to give child three choices to check against word and ask how they know that was right.	To use the book as an information text. To ask simple questions and use text to find answers.	is, a, big, he, for, will, get, no, not, too, going, where, up, with, and, down, good

Little Bulldozer

Story by Beverley Randell
Illustrations by Marina McAllan

Level: Yellow Set 3
Genre: Story with elements of fantasy
Running words: 170
Links to other PM titles: None

Overview

This story is reminiscent of *Baby Bear goes fishing* in its confirmation of the contribution small characters can make. Little Bulldozer's offers of help are turned down by other, larger vehicles until the big bulldozer invites him to help push down a tree. Remind your pupils of other titles with this theme (they may also recall *Football at the park*). Ask pupils to think of other animated story characters, such as *Thomas the Tank Engine*. The cartoon-like style of this storybook could easily be translated into a cartoon strip using speech bubbles.

Introducing the text

- Read the title and discuss what a bulldozer does.
- Look at page 4 and predict whether Little Bulldozer will be able to help the fire engine. Focus on the expressions of the characters, and how this is reinforced by what they say.
- Look at page 6, and discuss why the fire engine does not want Little Bulldozer to help.
- Discuss how Little Bulldozer is feeling on page 11, and predict what will happen next.
- Confirm predictions on pages 12 to 16.

Reading the text

- Encourage re-reading for self-correction.
- Observe the childrens use of picture cues and whether attempts at unknown words are being cross-checked with letter cues.
- Encourage the use of letter cues if 'truck' is a miscue on page 9.

Revisiting the text

- Discuss how Little Bulldozer felt when he was told to go away. Relate this to the children's experiences of being told to go away by older brothers or sisters.
- Discuss the opportunities the children have for helping at home and what they like to do.
- Revise the use of capital letters with particular reference to 'Fire Engine' on page 5.
- Use small whiteboards or paper, and ask the children to write 'help', 'helping', 'helped', and 'helps'.
- Read some of the text to the children and ask them to identify words with an 'l' sound in the word (not at the beginning), for example on page 5:
  'hello', 'will', 'bulldozer', 'help'

Writing activities

- Ask children to add another page to the end of the story describing how Little Bulldozer helps the big bulldozer with another job.
- Get the children to write about helping at home. Ensure that they plan their writing first, either using a frame like the one below, or by drawing pictures.

When	Who	Why

- Identify the toy vehicles in the classroom. Make the children write a caption describing the function of one of them, for example: The crane lifts things high in the air.

Poems, rhymes and jingles

The steam shovel

The steam digger
Is much bigger
Than the biggest beast I
  know,
He snorts and roars
Like the dinosaurs
That lived long years ago.
He crouches low
On his tractor paws
And scoops the dirt up
With his jaws,

Then swings his long
Stiff neck around
And spits it out
Upon the ground...
Oh, the steam digger
Is much bigger
Than the biggest beast I
  know,
He snorts and roars
Like the dinosaurs
That lived long years ago.

Rowena Bennett

Word level work	Sentence level work	Text level work	High-frequency words
To learn spellings with past and present tense endings, for example 'help', 'helping', 'helped', 'helps'.	To expect reading to make sense and check if it does not by matching the appearance of characters in the illustrations with what they are saying	To compare and contrast other stories with the theme of the contribution small characters can make. Look at other animated story characters.	this, is, little, went, to, look, at, a, said, I, like, will, help, you, go, away, the, going, are, too, he, big, play, come, with, tree, not, am

Sally's red bucket

Story by Beverley Randell
Illustrations by Meredith Thomas

Level: Yellow Set 3
Genre: Story with predictable language
Running words: 127
Links to other PM titles: *Sally and the daisy; Sally's beans; Sally and the sparrows*

Overview
Compare the setting of this title to the other Sally stories. This title could be used to talk about tides, and how these affect the wave pattern. You may also talk about safety at the beach. If Sally's little red bucket had been washed further out, would they still have gone out to fetch it? What about cross-currents? What sort of animal do you expect to see at the beach?

Introducing the text
- Read the title and discuss where the story takes place. Predict what might happen to Sally's bucket.
- Relate the story to children's experiences of going to the beach and playing in the waves.
- Ensure the children hear and locate the word 'waves'.
- Ensure on page 6 that the children notice the waves on the beach and the red bucket, and how close the waves are to Mum.
- Look at page 9 and predict who will see the red bucket.
- Look at page 12. Predict what will happen when Mum runs into the water. Refer the children back to page 6.

Reading the text
- Observe whether the children sound the 's' on 'Sally's'.
- If 'stay' is a difficult word, make a short letter string from 'day', for example 'day', 'play', 'stay'.
- Observe whether the children notice the letter change from 'come' to 'came'. If the children read 'come' for 'came', repeat what they said and ask, 'Does that sound right?'

Revisiting the text
- Retell the main events of the story.
- Revisit the story *Seagull is clever* and compare the use of the word 'waves'. Extend the children's vocabulary by asking them to describe the waves in both books.
- Make 'back' with magnetic letters and notice the 'ck' ending. Make a list of other words that end with the same two letters.
- Use magnetic letters to make the irregular verb 'come', 'coming' and the change of one letter to make 'came'.

Writing activities
- Ask the children to write instructions for making a sandcastle.
- Look at the illustration on page 2 and discuss how Sally is protecting her skin in the sun. Use this as a starting point to make a poster about keeping safe in the sun, for example:
    Keeping Safe in the Sun.
    Wear a hat in the sun.
- Using the illustration on page 14, ask the children to write down what happened when Mum and Sally went into the water.
- The children could write about what they like to do when they go to the seaside.

Poems, rhymes and jingles

At the sea-side

When I was down
Beside the sea
A wooden spade
They gave to me
To dig the sandy shore.
My holes were empty like a cup
In every hole the sea came up
Till it could come no more.

Robert Louis Stevenson

Word level work	Sentence level work	Text level work	High-frequency words
To spell common irregular words, for example 'come', 'came'.	To use awareness of grammar to decipher new or unfamiliar words, for example sounding the 's' on 'Sally's'.	To retell the main events of the story and look at significant incidents that happened to Sally and her Mum, using prediction skills.	in, the, with, a, red, come, and, play, me, my, ball, said, ran, I, will, here, came, up, away, went, back, look, she, help, little, Mum, can, see, your, on, to, get, too, they, you, are, no

A friend for little white rabbit

Story by Beverley Randell
Illustrations by Drew Aitken

Level: Yellow Set 3
Genre: Story with patterned language
Running words: 113
Links to other PM titles: *Little Bulldozer; The hungry kitten; A home for Little Teddy* (Thematic)

Overview

Little white rabbit is looking for a friend to play with him, but all the animals chase him away, until at last he finds a friend in little brown rabbit. This simple narrative using patterned, repetitive language allows the child to make predictions with confidence. The format of this story is familiar (*The hungry kitten; A home for Little Teddy; Little Bulldozer*), as is the vocabulary, which means that this text should be easily accessible to your less confident readers.

Introducing the text

- Read the title and ask the children to talk about their friends. Discuss why the little white rabbit wants a friend.
- When introducing page 2, ensure that the children hear or use 'please'.
- Look at page 3 and predict what the lamb will say.
- Whom will he ask next on page 5?
- Predict what the duck will say on page 7.
- Look at page 11 and predict what will happen next.
- Confirm predictions on pages 14 to 16.

Reading the text

- If 'please' is a difficult word, remind children of the book introduction, and what they decided the rabbit would say. Ask the children to re-read and say the first letters of 'please'.
- Observe whether the children have noticed the repetition on pages 6 and 10, and read with pace.
- Observe whether the children use the punctuation on page 10 if 'who' is a difficult word.

Revisiting the text

- Look at the illustration on page 11, and ask the children to describe how the little white rabbit is feeling.
- Discuss what sort of questions the two rabbits might ask in order to get to know each other. Provide question words as starting clues:
    where, what, when, can, would you?
- Re-read page 2, and ask the children to identify two words that begin the same way. Make a list of other words beginning with 'pl'.
- Revise adding 'ing' to verbs ending with 'e', for example:
    coming, liking, riding, hiding

Writing activities

- Ask the children to write an extra page for the story and describe the game the two rabbits played.
- Ask them to write about the games they play with their friends at home or at school.
- Draw a rabbit for the wall, and ask the children to write captions to go around it, for example:
    A rabbit lives in a hole (burrow).
    A rabbit has whiskers.
- Children write a personal response to a part of the story, for example:
    I think the duck was mean to the little white rabbit.
    I felt sad when the little white lamb said 'Go away'.

Poems, rhymes and jingles

White rabbit
I have a little rabbit
Whose ears are soft as silk
His eyes are round as saucers
And his coat as white as milk.
My rabbit cannot talk to me
But only twitch his nose,
I can tell when he is happy
As twitchety-twitch he goes.

Word level work	Sentence level work	Text level work	High-frequency words
To ensure that children can identify words that begin the same way, for example words beginning with 'pl'.	To read the text with pace and expression with awareness of grammar, for example raising the voice for questions.	To extend the story about the friendship of the two rabbits.	little, white, will, you, play, with, me, said, the, no, I, not, go, away, who, is, this, brown, yes, come, on

Fire! Fire!

Story by Beverley Randell
Illustrations by Crissie Davies

Level: Yellow Set 3
Genre: Story with predictable structure
Running words: 161
Links to other PM titles: None

Overview
The drama of this story about a bushfire which threatens the Brown's family home is made more immediate by the use of speech bubbles to relay the direct speech. Remind children of previous examples of speech bubbles (*Jolly Roger, the pirate*) and compare them with other conventions used for direct speech. The tension in this story is given an added twist when the family cat jumps out the helicopter and runs back to the house. The reader is left wondering not only whether the house will survive but whether Puss will escape the fire.

Introducing the text
- Read the title and discuss the cover illustration. Talk about helicopters, how they fly, and whether any of the children have been in one before.
- Discuss what the helicopter is doing and why a fire engine is not able to come. What special attributes does a helicopter have, and why was the family not rescued by plane? Discuss the word 'rescue'.
- Ensure the children understand that the speech bubbles develop the storyline.
- Look at page 2 and notice Dad calling the fire service on his mobile.
- Predict where the cat might go on page 8.

Reading the text
- Ensure the children read the 'straight text' before the speech bubbles.
- Observe whether the children read the speech bubbles with expression.
- If the word 'again' on page 12 is a difficulty, direct the children to letter cues.

Revisiting the text
- Why could the helicopter not wait for the Browns to find Puss?
- Role-play the story, then read as a play with the children saying the character parts from the speech bubbles.
- Allow children to retell the story in their own words.
- Use the classroom telephone for the children to role-play how to convey urgent messages.
- Play a form of 'hangman' with the group (see page 55 for the details).
- Find 'all' in the text on page 3. Make a list of other words ending with 'll' ('will' and 'bull' from *Little Bulldozer*).

Writing activities
- Decide on a different rescue scenario. For example, consider what would happen if someone were upstairs with a fire in the downstairs room. Ask the children to write their alternative solution.
- Ask children to draw four pictures with speech bubbles to tell the story.
- Get the children to role-play being one of the Browns who writes a thank-you card to the helicopter pilot.
- Re-write pages 4 and 5 as 'straight text' without speech bubbles.

Poems, rhymes and jingles

> **My helicopter**
> If I had a helicopter
> All of my own
> I'd keep it in the garden
> Where the cabbages are grown.
> I'd rise up every morning
> Without any fuss
> And wave to all my friends below
> Queuing for the bus.

Word level work	Sentence level work	Text level work	High-frequency words
To extend vocabulary by collecting new words about the text subject, for example 'helicopter', 'rescue'.	To read the speech bubbles with expression.	To look at speech bubbles and compare them with other conventions used for direct speech.	help, all, the, down, to, you, get, in, come, with, me, got, ran, away, no, back, up, we, go, went, out, going, and

A Lucky Day for Little Dinosaur

Story by Hugh Price
Illustrations by Ben Spiby

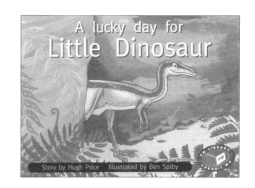

Level: Yellow Set 3
Genre: Story with predictable structure
Running words: 135
Links to other PM titles: None

Overview
This is a story about the adventures of Little Dinosaur. Ensure that the children grasp the scale of the illustrations, and are able to appreciate how large Little Dinosaur is by comparing him with the things he eats. This is another story about perspective: it may be a lucky day for Little Dinosaur, but it is an unlucky day for some of the other mini-beasts that appear in the story. Is it a lucky day for Big Dinosaur? What facts are the children able to glean from this story? As with all the 'science/nature' titles in the PM series, the information and illustrations are accurate.

Introducing the text
- Read the title and discuss the concept of luck.
- Relate being lucky to the children's experience.
- Ensure on page 2 that the children understand the dinosaur came out of a hole, not a cave.
- Ensure the children notice the writing in italics at the bottom of the pages, and how it relates to the dinosaur finding food.
- Look at page 12 and predict what Little Dinosaur will do.
- Ensure the children have all seen dinosaur's vanishing tail on page 16.

Reading the text
- Encourage self-correction if the children make an error by saying, 'You made a mistake/missed out a word/put in an extra word on that page. Read that bit again and look at……'
- Observe whether the children use the picture cues to read the nouns naming the insects.
- Observe how the children attempt to read the word 'dragonfly'. Encourage segmenting into chunks if it presents a difficulty.
- Encourage the children to highlight the excitement of the story by using the punctuation cues appropriately.

Responding to the text
- Discuss how Little Dinosaur was very lucky at the end.
- Ask the children to identify the part of the story they liked, and why.
- Use magnetic letters to add 'ing' and 'ed' to regular verbs such as 'look' and 'like'.
- Demonstrate the irregular verbs 'go' and 'come'.
- Segment and blend CVC words such as 'sit', 'sun', 'ran', and ask the children to write them.

Writing activities
- Get the children to write about Little Dinosaur's breakfast, as follows:
    First dinosaur ate …
    Then he ate …
    After that he ate …
    Next he ate …
- Using the illustrations and the information in the text to ask the children to write about dinosaurs, for example:
    Some dinosaurs were big.
    Some dinosaurs were little.
    Dinosaurs laid eggs.
    Some dinosaurs ate insects.
- Get the children to write about their own experiences of being lucky, for example:
    I am lucky because my Mum buys me ice-cream.
    I am lucky because Gran is coming to stay.

Poems, rhymes and jingles
Two Jurassic dinosaurs
Young Comsognathus
was much like a chicken
A dinosaur smaller than us,
But Megalosaurus
was truly enormous,
The height of a two-decker bus!
Beverley Randell

Word level work	Sentence level work	Text level work	High-frequency words
To add -ing and -ed to regular verbs. To look at irregular verbs 'go' and 'come'.	To encourage the child to build on the excitement of the story by using punctuation cues, for example: bold and italic writing, and exclamation marks.	To encourage children to identify the part of the story they liked and why.	little, came, out, of, his, he, went, to, in, the, brown, by, at, it, ran, after, and, got, day, for, green, on, a, tree, down, look, big, went, very

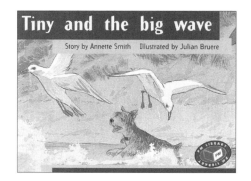

Tiny and the big wave

Story by Annette Smith
Illustrations by Julian Bruere

Level: Yellow Set 3
Genre: Story with predictable language
Running words: 155
Links to other PM titles: *Lucky goes to dog school* (Thematic)

Overview

If your children have read the PM Starters, they may remember the previous story about Tiny. Talk about other titles which feature a disobedient dog. (*Lucky goes to dog school*). Compare the setting with other seaside settings (*Sally's red bucket*; *Seagull is clever*). Ensure that pupils notice the information provided by the illustration on page 2. Talk about the sign and why it is important that dogs are kept on leads, i.e. to protect themselves and the environment. If your school has an environmental awareness programme, talk about the need to keep dogs under control. This story could be modelled to show its circular structure: the story begins and ends at the signpost, but because of what has happened, both Matt and Tiny are wiser than they were at the beginning.

Introducing the text

- Read the title and establish who Tiny is.
- On page 2, read the notice to the children, and predict what is going to happen.
- On pages 8 and 9, predict what the family will do.
- Confirm the prediction on page 11, and predict what will happen to Tiny.
- Confirm the predictions on pages 12 and 13, and predict what the family will do next.

Reading the text

- Observe how the children attempt to read 'seagulls'. Encourage segmenting into known words.
- If 'cried' is a difficult word on page 9, direct the child to say the first letters and think about how Matt would say 'Oh no!'
- Encourage the children to heighten the drama of the story through the different voices of the characters.

Responding to the text

- Discuss the emotions of Matt on pages 11 to 13.
- Discuss what the family will do next time they take Tiny for a walk.
- Play tic-tac-toe with the group using high-frequency words.
- Make 'cry' with magnetic letters. Add 'ing' and 'ed'. Ensure children can articulate the rule. Check it against other words the children know that end with 'y'.

Writing activities

- Using the illustration on pages 8 and 9, get the children to write a description of what happened to Tiny.
- Discuss the children's experiences of playing in the waves. Get the children to write about the waves.
- Ask the children to write a poem about waves using one adjective, for example:

   ... waves
   ... waves
   ... waves
   ... waves
   But last of all
   Best of all
   I like ... waves.

Word level work	Sentence level work	Text level work	High-frequency words
To look at the common spelling patterns of words that end with 'y'.	To use word order to help predict finding known and unknown words in a sentence.	To look at circular structure of the story. Highlight beginning and end at signpost and the significant events in the middle.	Mum, Dad, and, went, for, a, ran, all, the, way, down, to, come, back, here, is, your, after, she, said, away, up, water, big, came, on, no, where, look, with, me, at, he, I, can, see, out, get, her, going, home, too, dog

Snowy gets a wash

Story by Beverley Randell
Illustrations by Elspeth Lacey

Level: Yellow Set 3
Genre: Story with predictable structure
Running words: 181
Links to other PM titles: *The photo book; Wake up, Dad; The merry-go-round; The bumper cars; The flower girl; Hide and seek; Where are the sunhats?*

Overview
Review previous titles in this mini-series to see whether the children can see Snowy. Draw attention to the convention of narrating the story in the past tense, and how this compares with direct speech which is in the present tense. This is the last of the Yellow Set Storybooks, and children who are reading these with confidence will have a reading age of approximately 5½. They should have covered many of the NLS objectives outlined in Y1 Term 1 and Term 2, and some of the Term 3 objectives.

Introducing the text
- Read the title and discuss who Snowy is and why Nick is looking upset.
- Look at the illustration on the title page and ask the children whether it gives any clues as to why Snowy might need washing.
- Look at pages 2 to 6, and predict what is happening to Snowy.
- Predict what Mum is going to do on page 7.
- Discuss how Nick is feeling on page 11.
- Look at page 14 and discuss why Nick will not go inside.

Reading the text
- Observe whether the children use picture cues to confirm their decoding of 'white'.
- Direct the children to picture cues and letter cues to read grey.
- Observe whether the children are always attempting unfamiliar words.

Responding to the text
- Discuss how Nick feels about her teddy bear. Ask the children to find evidence in the text and illustrations to support their opinions.
- Re-read what Nick said on pages 8, 10 and 14. Ask the children to read it in Nick's anxious voice.
- Reinforce the long 'e' sound. Read the children passages from the text and ask them to clap when they hear a word with a long 'e' sound, for example on pages 5, 8, and 12.
- Play tic-tac-toe with the children. Get a child from the group to write a CVC word from the story such as 'can', 'get', 'not', 'pit', 'wet', 'sit', 'sun'. The teacher then writes a four letter word from the story such as 'with', 'here', 'said', 'help', 'back', 'look', 'come'.

Writing activities
- Look at Snowy's label on page 8. Compare it with labels on the children's clothes. Ask the children to write a label for one of the toys in the classroom, for example:
   Do Not Wash   Not For Babies   Wash Me
- Refer to the text to write about the things Nick liked to do:
   Nick liked to play in the sandpit.
   Nick liked to climb the tree.
- Ask the children to revisit the illustrations on pages 11 to 16 and write about Nick's feelings.
   Nick was … when … because …

Poems, rhymes and jingles

Teddy Bear
I have a little Teddy Bear
He is such a jolly fellow
His eyes are black
His nose is soft
and his coat is fluffy yellow.

Word level work	Sentence level work	Text level work	High-frequency words
To read on sight the high-frequency word specific to the child's ability.	To expect the reading to make sense and check if it does not.	To direct children to use a range of phonological, contextual, grammatical and graphic cues to help in making sense of what they are reading.	in, the, with, her, white, she, on, went, for, up, tree, down, again, and, came, out, a, of, at, your, is, not, said, he, grey, can, you, this, Mum, me, in, water, to, going, back, come, help, here, we, go, look, all, get, got

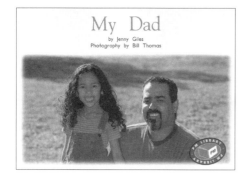

My Dad

Story by Jenny Giles
Photography by Bill Thomas

Level: Yellow; non-fiction
Genre: Observation recounts
Running words: 113
Links to other PM titles: Other Yellow non-fiction titles

Overview

To facilitate easy reading of the non-fiction titles, it will be necessary for the child to make links both with Red level non-fiction texts and with the Yellow level story book texts. Remind children of the language of comparison (bigger than/smaller than) introduced in *Tall Things*. What other Dad was good at cooking sausages? (Tom's Dad in *Sausages*) Compare settings (beach/home), and more abstract concepts such as helping each other (*Baby Bear goes fishing*).

Introducing the text

- Read the title. Talk about why Dad is crouched down in the photograph on the cover and the title page.
- Compare the size of Dad and the girl. Compare the size of clothes, feet, hands, and so on.
- Discuss the way they are dressed and what time of year it is.
- On pages 6 and 7, discuss where the family is going and what they will do.
- On page 11, refer to *Sausages* where Dad and Tom cooked sausages for Mum.

Reading the text

- On page 2, 'very' may present decoding difficulties. Ask a question which directs the children to think about how big Dad is, and ask them to cross-check answers with the initial letter.
- Observe whether the children are using the picture and visual cues together to read 'shoes' before 'hats' on page 4.
- On page 7, some children may struggle with 'way'. Tell them to compare it with 'day' and change the first letter.
- If 'waves' on page 8 is substituted for another word (for example 'water'), cover the word and say, 'It could be. That makes sense, but what sound can you hear in the middle of 'water'?' Uncover the word and let the child see that there is no 't'. Say, 'Think of another word that means the same with a 'v' sound in the middle.'

Revisiting the text

- On pages 14 to 16, talk about the things the father and his daughter did to help each other. Discuss how the children help at home.
- Look at pages 6 and 7. Discuss what the family is wearing or carrying that will protect them from the sun.
- Discuss the illustration on page 9 from a water safety point of view.
- Make 'playhouse' with magnetic letters. Ask the children to make it into two words. Refer to 'into' used in previous texts. What other compound words do the children know?
- Find all the words that end with 'ing' in the text.
- Ask the children to find 'play' on page 8. Find other words in the text that rhyme, like 'day', 'way'. Make a word string.

Writing activities

- Make a 'helping' book or wall story, for example:
  I help ... to ... and ... helps me to ...
- Make a simple 'water safety' wall story, for example:
  My ... watches me.
  I go in the water with my ...
  Each child could write a page.
- Make a simple 'sun safety' poster with a slogan such as 'Be safe in the sun!'. Get the children to draw items with a caption to stick on, for example 'Wear a hat!'

Word level work	Sentence level work	Text level work	High Frequency words
To use initial and medial letter sounds to make sense of a word, for example waves and water.	To notice that 'Dad' and 'Mum' start with a capital letter.	To study Dad and the girl, comparing size of clothes, feet, hands, and so on, looking at the way they are dressed.	Mum, Dad, is, in, the

Our Mum

Story by Jenny Giles
Photography by Bill Thomas

Level: Yellow; non-fiction
Genre: Observation recounts
Running words: 120
Links to other PM titles: Other Yellow non-fiction titles

Overview

Ensure that your children realise who is telling this story, and compare what they know about this family to the family in *My Dad*. What is similar about the things that this family does, and the activities described in *My Dad*? (Draw attention to the similar emphasis placed on safety: in *My Dad* the family wears sunhats, in this title Mum oversees the children playing on the swings.) Can they remember what other character fell over and needed Mum to see to grazed knees? (Tom in *Tom is brave*) How do your children know that the children in the book love their Mum and that she loves them?

Introducing the text

- Read the title and discuss what the children and their mother are doing on the front cover and on the title page.
- Explain that kindergarten is the same as nursery.
- Discuss why Mum is sitting close to the swings on page 7.
- Look at page 8. Use the word 'library' in a question. Ask the children to find the word in the text. Ask them to explain how they know that word says 'library' (because it starts with 'l' and has a 'b').

Reading the text

- Reinforce 'our' by referring to the title.
- Observe whether the child is cross-checking the predictions on page 10 by using the picture cues and letter cues.
- If 'inside' is a difficult word, ask the children to find a known word at the beginning ('in'). Ask the children to re-read the sentence and think about where the characters went.

Revisiting the text

- Discuss Mum's job at the nursery (kindergarten) and the children's own experience of nursery.
- Discuss the family's visit to the library and the children's favourite stories.
- Segment and blend 'bag'. Ask the children to write the initial, medial and final letters.
- Make 'bag' with magnetic letters. Change the final letter to make new words: bag, ban, bat, bad.
- Ask the children to write all the high-frequency words they know in a set period of time. Use the high-frequency words from the text as a prompt, such as: her, to, get, up, the, we, go, like, likes, and, at.

Writing activities

- Discuss some things the children's mothers do. Help the children to turn this into an 'our Mum' book or wall story:
    My Mum goes to work.
    My Mum brings me to school.
- Ask the children to write a book review of a favourite book:
    I like … because …
  Use the reviews to promote the book corner.
- Ask the children to make a card for Mum.
- Ask them to make a list of the things Mum does at home such as cooking or looking after pets.

Word level work	Sentence level work	Text level work	High-frequency words
To find a word and use initial, medial or final letter sounds to work out the word, for example 'library' – 'l', 'b', 'y'.	If a word is difficult, to encourage the child to look at part of word, re-read the sentence and think about what would fit.	To compare the family in the story to the family in *My Dad*.	Mum, our, is, in, the, a, she, at, little, sister, with, go, school, play, can, see

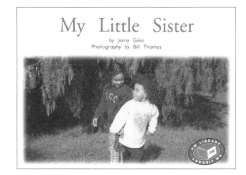

My Little Sister

Story by Jenny Giles
Photography by Bill Thomas

Level: Yellow non-fiction, 'Families around us'
Genre: Observational recounts
Running words: 118
Links to other PM titles: Other Yellow non-fiction titles

Overview
This text provides a useful contrast and parallel text to *My Big Brother*. The children could consider the different perspective that the two texts adopt by contrasting and comparing the comparative language on page 4 of this book with page 2 in *My Big Brother*. Note the similarity of the last pages of the two titles and also the emphasis placed in both texts on the sense of responsibility the older sibling shows towards the younger. As always with the early non-fiction texts, it is crucial that children relate the experiences they read about to their own life.

Introducing the text
- Find out how many in the group have sisters. Discuss the things these children do together.
- Look at the cover and the title page. Identify the older sister and the 'little sister' from the title.
- Look at page 3. Discuss the features that make the children look alike, for example: eyes, hair, similar smile.
- Discuss what the children are playing with in the sandpit on page 9.

Reading the text
- If 'after school' is a difficult phrase for the child to read at the beginning of the sentence, ask the children to think about when the big sister can play with her little sister. Give three choices which the child can check against the words to see if they look right, for example 'before school', 'on Saturday', or 'after school'.
- Observe if the children are using the pictures to check the predictions on page 8.
- Observe if the children cross-check picture cues with initial letters to read the names of the toys on page 10.

Revisiting the text
- Revisit the illustration on page 11. Discuss how the sisters have made their playhouse. Discuss whether the children do this at home.
- On page 13 we discover the big sister is reading *The Smallest Turtle* by Lynley Dodd. Discuss what the children's choices would have been. Discuss any other stories by Lynley Dodd that the children may have heard of such as *Hairy McClary from Donaldson's Dairy*, or *My Cat Likes to Hide in Boxes*.
- Discuss what games the children like to play with their brothers and sisters.
- Segment and blend 'big'. Ask the children to write the initial, medial and final sounds.
- Make 'big' with the magnetic letters. Change the medial vowel to make new words: big, bag, bug, beg.

Writing activities
- Ask the children to write another page for the text. Plan it using a writing frame along the lines:

When	Where	What	Who
After school	At home	Lego	Big sister

Alternatively, the children could draw pictures instead of using words on their own plans before turning it into a sentence.

- Using the information in the book, ask the children to make a character study of the little sister, such as:

    The little sister is 3 …
    She likes to …
    She looks like …

- Let the children write instructions on how to build a sandcastle, for example:

    Get a bucket and spade.
    Fill the bucket with sand.

Word level work	Sentence level work	Text level work	High-frequency words
To look at common spelling patterns by making word strings using b-g.	To offer choices of phrases for children to check against a difficult phrase to see if they look right.	To compare and contrast the language and content with *My Big Brother*. Discuss preferences.	my, little, sister, like, me, and, I, look, big, is, school, play

My Big Brother

Story by Jenny Giles
Photography by Bill Thomas

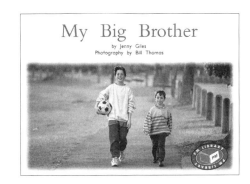

Level: Yellow non-fiction, 'Families around us'
Genre: Observational recounts
Running words: 103
Links to other PM titles: Other Yellow non-fiction titles

Overview

This text works in tandem with *My Little Sister*. Discuss the probable age of both narrators, and why in one the narrator describes herself as 'big', and in the other the narrator describes himself as 'little'. Look closely at the photographs, and allow pupils to speculate about the subtext on pages 14 to 16 based on the expressions and body language. Is there a narrative structure and sequence to these stories? Allow pupils to experiment by making copies of the story and then cutting them up. (Some pages are linked through content, and the first and last pages should retain their position, but the other pages could be reordered.) Compare this with one of the storybooks, and reinforce the conclusions reached.

Introducing the text

- Read the title. Compare the first page with that of *My Little Sister*. Discuss whether the two boys look the same.
- Discuss the difference in size between the two brothers on page 3 and the difference in their bikes on pages 5 to 7.
- Ensure that the children understand and can read the word 'fort' on page 10.
- Discuss who owns the big red truck on page 12 and how the big brother lets the little brother play with it.

Reading the text

- Observe whether the children read the changes between 'I', 'We', and 'He' accurately at the beginning of sentences.
- If 'our' presents a difficulty on page 4, ask a question related to the meaning, for example, 'Whose bikes are we riding?', or give choices such as:
  We like to ride my bike
  We like to ride our bikes
  We like to ride their bikes
- If a child struggles with the word 'games' on page 8, ask him/her to re-read and say the first letter and think about what would make sense? (I play g…)
- Observe whether the child is using the picture cues to read page 14 accurately.

Revisiting the text

- Look at the illustrations on pages 14 and 15. Discuss what the brothers might be saying to each other. Relate it to the last page – how is the big brother looking after the little brother?
- Discuss the games the children like to play with their brothers or sisters.
- Make 'bike' from magnetic letters. Change to 'like', add 's', 'ing' and 'ed' to both 'bike' and 'like'.
- Add 'inside' on page 12 to the class's growing list of compound words.

Writing activities

- Ask the children to use the information from the text to write about big brother, for instance:
  Big brother is 9
  He likes to play football
  He likes to ride his bike
- Get the children to make a wall display of games they like to play. It could be divided into games at home and games at school.
- Ask them to to write an 'at the park' story using a writing frame similar to the one below.

When	Where	Who
After school	On the swings	My mum and me

Word level work	Sentence level work	Text level work	High-frequency words
To learn spellings with 'ed' and 'ing' endings, for example using 'like' and 'bike'.	To see the changes between 'I', 'We', and 'He' at the beginning of sentences.	To investigate to see if there is narrative structure and sequence in the story.	My, big, brother, is, and, I, am, little, we, like, to

Our Baby

Story by Jenny Giles
Photography by Bill Thomas

Level: Yellow non-fiction, 'Families around us'
Genre: Observation recounts
Running words: 91
Links to other PM titles: Other Yellow non-fiction titles

Overview

Re-read *The new baby* and encourage pupils to talk about their own experiences of having a baby in the family. This story is narrated by the baby's two brothers – an assumption that the children should be able to infer from the use of first person plural pronouns in the narrative voice. The children should use the photographs to expand on the information provided by the text. (For instance, the reader uses the photographs to find out whether the baby is a boy or a girl. The photographs also show how the grandparents feel about the baby.)

Introducing the text

- Read the title, and name the family members on the cover and the title page. Discuss how the two boys have one sister. One of the boys has one brother and one sister. The baby has two brothers.
- Ensure the children understand the text is told by both boys, hence 'our' and 'we'.
- On page 5, predict why Mum has come into the room.
- Ensure 'clever' is used in a question, for example on page 8. Ask the children to find 'clever' in the text.

Reading the text

- If the children have difficulty beginning to read on pages 2 to 4, refer back to the title and compare the title to the first words on pages 2 to 4.
- Look at page 6. 'Teeth' cannot be predicted from the picture. Ask a question related to the meaning of the word, for example, 'What could we see in the baby's mouth?'. Ask the children to cross-check using initial or medial letters.
- If 'clever' on page 8 presents a difficulty, ask the children to re-read and say the first sound 'cl....'.
- If the children struggle with reading 'us' on page 10, ask 'Who is the baby playing with?' and then make them re-read the first sentence quickly.

Revisiting the text

- Discuss the things a baby is able to do and what the family has to do for the baby.
- Discuss the grandparents and any visits the children have with their own grandparents.
- Look at the baby's toys on page 11. Discuss how babies' toys are different from their own (no sharp edges, loose wheels, etc.).
- Revise adding 'ing', 's', 'ed', to 'like', 'look', 'play'.
- Look at page 6. Make 'feed' and 'see' with magnetic letters. Discover which sounds are similar. Get the children to find another word on the page with the same sound.

Writing activities

- Ask the children to use the photograph on page 5 to write speech bubbles for the characters.
- Get them to make a 'yes and no' book by completing the sentence 'Can a baby …?' The answer should be written under a flap. Ensure that some of the children write things a baby cannot do. Share the book with the rest of the class.
- Ask the children to draw a picture of a baby for the wall using the information in the text to make captions, for example:
    A baby has little teeth.
    A baby sleeps in a cot.
    A baby sits in a high chair.
Or they could make a wall story of things a baby likes to do, for example:
    A baby likes to play with toys.
    A baby likes to have a bath.

Word level work	Sentence level work	Text level work	High-frequency words
To segment words into phonemes for reading.	To look at a sentence as a whole for cues to decipher unfamiliar words.	To look at the title page and cover to help predict content. To become aware of the use of photographs to expand on the information given by the text.	our, is, up, and, she, her, like, can

My Gran and Grandad

Story by Jenny Giles
Photography by Bill Thomas

Level: Yellow non-fiction, 'Families around us'
Genre: Observation recounts
Running words: 129
Links to other PM titles: Other Yellow non-fiction titles

Overview

Draw attention to any fictional titles you are reading which feature grandparents. (Think back to *The new baby*.) Compare the activities that this child does with his grandparents with the activities described in the other books. Talk about the common themes in the 'family' series (looking after and being looked after, helping and being helped, loving and being loved, and so on). Discuss why we need families, and how people belong to different kinds of family. Talk about the different family configurations that your pupils come from.

Introducing the text

- Read the title. Discuss the different names the children call their grandparents.
- Discuss the times the children may have stayed with their grandparents or somebody else. Discuss what they do when they stay there.
- Ensure that the children notice the teddy on page 5.
- Ensure the children understand what the boy and his grandparents are doing on pages 12 and 13.

Reading the text

- Observe whether the child notices the ending 'dad' which changes 'Gran' to 'Grandad'.
- Observe whether the children use picture cues on page 4.
- If the word 'makes' presents a difficulty, compare it with 'cakes' on page 8.
- Observe whether the children use picture cues to read page 14.

Revisiting the text

- Discuss why the boy likes staying with his grandparents.
- Discuss the relationship between the boy's parents and the grandparents.
- Make a word string of words ending with the same letter cluster as 'kick'.
- List words beginning with the same letter cluster as 'gran'.

Writing activities

- Make a list of the names the children call their grandparents.
- Ask the children to draw or paint pictures of their grandparents and write a caption, such as:
    This is …
    Here is …
- Ask your children to imagine that they are the boy in the story. Tell them to write a 'thank-you' letter to their grandparents for looking after them.
- Discuss how Gran made the cakes and then ask the children to write a simple recipe, such as:
    Using butter, flour, eggs, milk.
    Put in the butter.
    Put in the eggs (and so on).

Word level work	Sentence level work	Text level work	High-frequency words
To look at different names the children call their grandparents.	To show how the names of the children's grandparents start with a capital letter.	To look at the common themes in the 'family' series. Discuss which book they like best. Talk about the children's families.	I, am, going, to, with, and, my, Mum, Dad

Assessment checklist

Name: _____   Age: _____

Skills	Comment	Date
Participates confidently in shared reading.		
Participates confidently in shared writing.		
Can sit and listen to stories.		
Can sit and read a book with a friend.		
Can retell a known story.		
Can read print in the environment.		
Understands that print conveys a message.		
Assigns meaning to own writing.		
Knows where to start reading.		
Knows when a book is upside down.		
Can indicate the front and back cover of a book.		
Knows to read left page before right.		
Can indicate which way to go on more than one line of print.		
Can point one to one when the teacher is reading.		
Can point one to one when reading.		
Can find a word.		
Can find a letter.		
Can find the space between words.		
Attitudes		
Enjoys and uses rhyme, rhythm and alliteration in language.		
Participates eagerly in the reading of stories, rhymes and poems.		
Expects books to make sense both when reading and being read to.		
Considers himself/herself a reader and expects others to do so.		

© PM Red/Yellow Teacher's Guide. Published by Nelson 2000. This page may be photocopied for educational use within purchasing institution.

Reading record

Name: _____ Age: _____ Date: _____

Text: **Where is Hannah?** _____ Level: _____ R. W.: _132_

Accuracy: _____ S. C. Rate: _____

Page		E	S. C.	Errors MSV	Self corrections MSV
2	Hannah and Mum went to the gym.				
4	"Oh! Look, Mum!" said Hannah. "I can see a trampoline, and look at the rope and the ladders."				
6	"Come and look at me, Mum! I can go up and down on the trampoline," said Hannah. Hannah went up and down, up and down, up and down.				
8	"Look at me! I'm on the rope," said Hannah. "Come and look at me, Mum. I can swing on the rope."				
10	Mum went away to look at the notices. Hannah looked at the ladder. "I can go up ladders," said Hannah.				
12	Hannah went up the ladder. She went up, and up, and up. Mum looked for Hannah. She looked at the rope. She went to the trampoline.				
14	"Hannah! **Hannah!** Where are you?" said Mum. Hanna looked down at Mum.				
	TOTAL				

Example of an Assessment Record © Nelson, 2000. This page may be photocopied for educational use within the purchasing institution.

Reading record

Name: _____ **Age:** _____ **Date:** _____

Text: Snowy gets a wash **Level:** _____ **R. W.:** 132

Accuracy: _____ **S. C. Rate:** _____

Page		E	S. C.	Errors MSV	Self corrections MSV
2	Nick liked playing in the garden with her white teddy bear. She liked swinging on the swing.				
3	She liked playing in the sandpit.				
4	Snowy went for rides on Nick's truck.				
5	Snowy went up in the tree with Nick.				
6	Snowy went down the slide with Nick, again and again.				
7	Mum came out with a basket of washing. She looked at Snowy. "Your teddy bear is not **white**," she said. "He is **grey**."				
8	Mum and Nick looked at Snowy. "Can you read this, Nick?" said Mum. Wash me in cold water. Nick said to Snowy, "Mum is going to **wash** you!"				
10	Mum went inside, and came back with a bucket. "Come and help me, Nick," she said. "Here we go. Look! The water is going grey." "Snowy is all wet," said Nick. "Oh, Snowy!"				
	TOTAL				

Example of an Assessment Record © Nelson, 2000.   This page may be photocopied for educational use within the purchasing institution.

Work planning guide/NLS Correlation to term-by-term objectives*

RED LEVEL (Set 1)

Title	Genre	Word level work	NLS	Sentence level work	NLS	Text level work	NLS	Writing extension	NLS
The photo book	Story with a predictable structure	Sight reading familiar high-frequency words and children's names.	R5	Convention of using capital letter to indicate names.	R4	Understanding words such as cover, author, title.	R1	Using phrases from the text, they could write a sentence under each 'photo'.	R1
Hedgehog is hungry	Story with a predictable structure	Recognition of grapheme/phoneme correspondence 'Hh'.	R2	To expect the story to make sense and to use picture cues for meaning.	R1	Track the text in the right order, page by page and from left to right.	R1	Make a group book of children's food preferences.	R1
Wake up, Dad	Story with a predictable structure	Read high-frequency words used in text.	R7	Use of grammar to predict words.	R2	Encourage children to be aware of story structure and how, in this story, structure is linked to Dad's refusal to get up.	R9	Use the picture on p3 and describe what is happening.	R9
Tiger, Tiger	Story with a predictable structure	Recognition of initial phoneme/grapheme correspondence in <u>T</u>iger, <u>B</u>aby, and <u>M</u>onkey.	R2	Children to check text to ensure that what has been read makes sense.	R1	Read and recite poem *Walking through the Jungle* and experiment with rhyming patterns.	R10	Use the structure of the story to write a sequel.	R10
The lazy pig	Story with a predictable structure	Long 'oo' sound.	Y1 (1) 8	Reading animal sounds with appropriate expression.	Y1 (1)	Linking personal experience to events in the story.	Y1 (1) 5	In a shared writing exercise, list sounds made by farm animals.	Y1 (1) 5
The merry-go-round	Story with familiar setting	Developing sight reading skills of children's names.	Y1 (1)	Reading with appropriate expression.	Y1 (1) 3	Applying word level skills through Guided Reading.	Y1 (1) 1	Write a recount of the children's experiences at a fair.	Y1 (1) 1
The little snowman	Story with familiar setting	Practise and secure alphabetic knowledge by helping children to self-correct over possible confusion of similar words such as 'snowman' and 'snowball'.	Y1 (1) 2	Use appropriate expression by encouraging children to read 'like talking'.	Y1 (1) 3	Use phonological, contextual, grammatical and graphic knowledge to work out, predict and to make sense of what they are reading.	Y1 (1) 2	Children draw a snowman with a different hat and write captions.	Y1 (1) 2
A birthday cake for Ben	Story with familiar setting	To recognise the critical features of words such as endings of 'look', 'looking' and 'looks'.	Y1 (1) 10	To expect reading to make sense.	Y1 (1) 1	Use phonological, contextual, grammatical and graphic knowledge to work out, predict and make sense of what they read.	Y1 (1) 2	Make birthday cards.	Y1 (1) 2

* Y1 = Year 1   (1) = Term 1   8 = NLS objective 8

RED LEVEL (Set 2)

Title	Genre	Word level work	NLS	Sentence level work	NLS	Text level work	NLS	Writing extension
Baby Lamb's first drink	Story with predictable language	To recognise common spelling patterns such as words beginning like 'sheep'.	Y1 (1) 10	Reading to make sense and to read aloud using expression such as use of the word 'Baa'.	Y1 (1) 3	To describe the spring setting of the story and relate them to child's own experience of spring.	Y1 (1) 5	Write a book about Spring.
Sally and the daisy	Story with familiar language	To hear and say phonemes in the final position. Link to games outlined in 'Progression in phonics'.	Y1 (1) 3	Encouraging use of punctuation on page 13 to read with expression.	Y1 (1) 3	To discuss the time frame of the story and what happened to Sally and the plant.	Y1 (1) 5	Make a story into a simple sequence.
The big kick	Story with predictable language	To investigate and recognise word patterns, for example 'look', 'looked', 'looking' and 'looks'.	Y1 (1) 10	Look at how words are used for emphasis in the story through repetition or by bold emphasis.	Y1 (1) 3	To reinforce and apply their word level skills through Shared and Guided Reading.	Y1 (1) 1	Innovate on the story to introduce position words.
Sausages	Story with predictable language	To investigate and learn spellings of words with 's' for plurals, for example 'sausages', 'horses'.	Y1 (2) 8	Using expression appropriate to grammar of text, for example how narrative of *Sausages* is entirely by direct speech.	Y1 (2) 1	To choose and read familiar stories, to discuss, for example the similarities between the covers of this story and *The big kick*.	Y1 (2) 3	Re-write the text as a simple sequence.
Pussy and the birds	Story with patterned language	To secure identification, spelling and reading of medial sounds, for example 'ee'.	Y1 (2) 1	To predict words from preceding sentences. For example, use meaning cue to read 'miaow'.	Y1 (2) 3	To identify and discuss characters, for example the cat. Compare with other texts about hungry animals.	Y1 (2) 8	Make lists about the likes of a cat.
The baby owls	Story with predictable language	Notice the plurals in the story with 's', for example cows, pigs, dogs, owls.	Y1 (2) 8	Draw attention to the speech bubble on page 4 and relate it to words in italics on page 12.	Y1 (2) 1	Encourage children's cross-checking skills by using picture cues and initial letters to read the names of the animals.	Y1 (2) 2	Make a 'sleep/not asleep' book using the children's names and animals they know who hunt at night.
The bumper cars	Story with a familiar setting	To secure identification, spelling and reading of initial letter sounds in simple words.	Y1 (2) 1	To use awareness of grammar to decipher new and unfamiliar words.	Y1 (2) 2	To identify and discuss the four characters and how they behave and are described in the text.	Y1 (2) 8	Use illustration on p15. Make a speech bubble for Dad and Nick.
The flower girl	Story with predictable language	New words from reading and shared experiences, for example words about weddings.	Y1 (2) 10	To predict words from preceding words.	Y1 (2) 3	To discuss reasons for, or causes of, incidents in stories, for example discussion of why she is angry.	Y1 (2) 7	Write a caption to a photobook of the wedding.

RED LEVEL (Set 3)

Title	Genre	Word level work	NLS	Sentence level work	NLS	Text level work	NLS	Writing extension
Ben's Teddy Bear	Story with predictable structure	Extend vocabulary by discussing new words to describe Ben's feelings	Y1 (2) 10	To use punctuation and bold print to ensure the child is reading with expression.	Y1 (2) 1	Deriving meaning from the relationship between text and illustration to help predict and make sense of what the child is reading.	Y1 (2) 2	Make a 'teddy bear' book.
Ben's treasure hunt	Story with predictable structure	Read on sight high-frequency words written with both upper and lower case letters.	Y1 (2) 4	Review the use of capital letters for names and for the start of a sentence.	Y1 (2) 7	Use range of problem-solving strategies in deriving meaning from text, such as looking at the interdependence of text and illustration in the story.	Y1 (2) 2	Make a 'What am I?' book with clues and a picture under a flap.
Lizard loses his tail	Story with predictable structure	Recognise the critical features of words, for example common spelling patterns with 'ing' endings.	Y1 (2) 7	To expect reading to make sense and check if it does not.	Y1 (2)	To identify and compare basic story elements, for example, compare and contrast this story with other Red level stories about the feeding habits of animals.	Y1 (2) 10	Innovate on 'Brown Bear, Brown bear'.
Father Bear goes fishing	Story with a fantasy setting	To identify and compare basic story elements, for example compare and contrast this story with other Red level stories about the feeding habits of animals.	Y1 (2) 3	To predict words from preceding words in sentences.	Y1 (2) 3	Reinforce and apply their word-level skills through Shared and Guided Reading.	Y1 (2) 1	Children write their own version of the story in sequence.
Tom is brave	Story with a familiar setting	To read on sight approximately 30 more high-frequency words.	Y1 (2) 6	Read with expression. e.g. use of bold print for exclamation.	Y1 (2) 1	To discuss reasons for, or causes of, incidents in the story about Tom.	Y1 (2) 7	Write a shopping list for Tom to take to the shops.
Hide and seek	Story with a familiar setting	To secure identification, spelling and reading of initial, final and medial letter sounds in simple words.	Y1 (2) 1	To expect reading to make sense and check if it does not.	Y1 (2) 1	By highlighting the ellipses encourage the child to notice difference between written and spoken forms of writing.	Y1 (2) 4	Write another page for the text where Dad goes to hide.
A home for Little Teddy	Story with patterned language	To investigate and learn spellings of words with 's' for plurals, for example 'rabbits' and 'dolls'.	Y1 (2) 8	To expect reading to make sense and check if it does not.	Y1 (2) 1	To use some of the elements in the story to write another page where Little Teddy asks someone else before the dolls.	Y1 (2) 16	Write a poem about Teddy Bears, using adjectives.
Where is Hannah?	Story with a predictable setting	To discriminate, read and spell words with initial consonant clusters, for example 'sw'.	Y1 (2) 3	To use awareness of grammar of a sentence to decipher new and unfamiliar words. e.g. 'trampoline' and 'rope'	Y1 (2) 2	To reinforce and apply their word-level skills through Shared and Guided Reading	Y1 (2) 1	Write an action poem.

RED LEVEL (Non-fiction)

Title	Genre	Word level work	NLS	Sentence level work	NLS	Text level work	NLS	Writing extension
Eggs for Breakfast	Story with information	For Guided Reading to read on sight high-frequency words such as 'here', 'this', 'we' without hesitation.	Y1 (2) 4	To expect reading to make sense and check if it does not.	Y1 (2) 1	To identify and discuss the family in the story.	Y1 (2) 8	Make a list of family members.
Red and Blue and Yellow	Story with information	Recognise common spelling patterns by making rhyming strings, for example from 'red'.	Y1 (2) 7	Predict text from the grammar. Re-read and check the child is reading all the words, for example 'school' and 'bag'.	Y1 (2) 2	To identify and discuss the style of non-fiction texts, for example, who is telling the story, the settings, the style of narrative.	Y1 (2) 10	Make a 'favourite colour' book.
Look Up, Look Down	Story with information	Investigate and revise words with initial consonant clusters, for example 'sw' and 'ch'.	Y1 (2) 3	Read with expression using the bold print as a cue.	Y1 (2) 1	Re-tell the story using the words 'first', 'then', 'next', and 'finally'. Look at the main points in sequence.	Y1 (2) 4	Make a 'down' and 'up' book.
A Roof and a Door.	Story with information	To read and spell words with final consonant clusters, for example 'th'.	Y1 (2) 3	To check if the child reads fluently using bold print for emphasis.	Y1 (2) 1	To use a variety of cues to work out, predict and check the meanings of unfamiliar words in the story.	Y1 (2) 2	Make a 'shape' book.
Tall Things	Story with information	Make word strings using words such as 'things' and 'crane'.	Y1 (2) 3	Encourage re-reading for self correction and for text to make sense.	Y1 (2) 3	Discuss reasons why various objects or people are tall or small in the book. Note shape of book.	Y1 (2) 7	Write a sentence based on p10.
Two Eyes, Two Ears	Story with information	Looking at new words from reading and shared experiences through the story subject of clothes and the body.	Y1 (2) 10	Use picture cues and cross-checking of letter cues to read words such as 'hands' and 'arms' accurately.	Y1 (2) 1	Identify and discuss the boy and his actions.	Y1 (2) 8	Make a 'brother' book.

YELLOW LEVEL (Set 1)

Title	Genre	Word level work	NLS	Sentence level work	NLS	Text level work	NLS	Writing extension	NLS
Where are the sunhats?	Story with predictable language.	To recognise compound words and list a variety connected to the text, for example 'inside' and compound words that have 'sun'.	Y1 (2) 7	To use punctuation in a sentence to decipher new or unfamiliar words, for example the strategies the child uses to read 'where' on page 2.	Y1 (2) 2	To build character profiles of the children based on the knowledge collected whilst reading the other titles about the family.	Y1 (2) 2	Rewrite a part of the story. Change 'sunhats' to 'woolly hats'.	Y1 (2) 8
Blackberries	Story with elements of fantasy	To use through reading and spelling initial, final and medial letter sounds in simple words using games such as hangman.	Y1 (2) 1	To notice the question marks in the text to help the child read accurately.	Y1 (2) 2	To compare and contrast the Bear family with other animal or non-animal families that appear in other titles.	Y1 (2) 2	Use illustration on p.8 and add speech bubbles.	Y1 (2) 10
Brave Father Mouse	Story with predictable structure	To discriminate, read and spell words with the initial consonant cluster 'br', for example 'bread', 'brave'.	Y1 (2) 3	To use the build-up of tension in the story to read expressively.	Y1 (2) 1	By looking at the sequence of events, discuss the reasons and causes why the reader's sympathies lie with the mouse and not the cat.	Y1 (2) 1	Rewrite the story as a comic strip, making a sequence of 4 pictures.	Y1 (2) 7
Mumps	Story with predictable language	Extend the child's vocabulary by learning and reading the days of the week.	Y1 (2) 10	To read direct speech in the way the characters would say it.	Y1 (2) 1	To re-tell the story, and to understand the sequence of the story through the days of the week.	Y1 (2) 1	Make a diary chart for a week in school.	Y1 (2) 4
The hungry kitten	Story with predictable language	Look at lists of sounds represented by letters, for example 'Grr', 'Sh-sh', 'Choo-choo'.	Y1 (2) 1	To use the tension in the story to read with expression.	Y1 (2) 1	Use a range of phonological, contextual, grammatical and graphic cues to work out, predict and check meanings of words within the text.	Y1 (2) 1	Write instructions on how to look after a pet.	Y1 (2) 2
Sally's beans	Story with familiar language	To read on sight the high-frequency words specific to the book.	Y1 (2) 4	Notice the bold text to help read with expression.	Y1 (2) 7	To discuss Sally as a character. From this story and the other story what does Sally enjoy doing? What is Sally doing to the plants in this story?	Y1 (2) 7	Write a bean poem using a known format.	Y1 (2) 8
Baby Hippo	Story with predictable structure	Look at the plurals in the text, focusing in those ending with 's'.	Y1 (2) 8	To predict words from preceding words in sentences to make sense of text.	Y1 (2) 3	To choose and read other books on similar theme of parental protection. To discuss preferences and give reasons.	Y1 (2) 3	Write about how children's parents/carers keep them safe.	Y1 (2) 3
Jolly Roger, the pirate.	Story with predictable structure	To look at all the words in the text with a long 'e' sound.	Y1 (2) 7	To read the speech 'like talking' and to notice how direct speech is shown by the speech bubbles.	Y1 (2) 1	To re-tell the story giving the main points in sequence and to notice the difference between written and spoken forms in re-telling.	Y1 (2) 1	Write a letter to Jolly Roger telling him how to avoid having his clothes stolen.	Y1 (2) 4

YELLOW LEVEL (Set 2)

Title	Genre	Word level work	NLS	Sentence level work	NLS	Text level work	NLS	Writing extension
Lucky goes to dog school	Story with predictable structure	Use final and medial letter sounds in simple words taken from the text, for example words ending with 'y', and changing medial vowels to make new words.	Y1 (2) 1	Use character's frustration with Lucky to read with expression.	Y1 (2) 1	Compare Lucky's behaviour at the beginning of the story and at the end. What happens in the middle to make the ending possible?	Y1 (2) 10	Rewrite story in own words, putting story into sequence.
Ben's dad	Story with predictable structure	Extend vocabulary by listing words to describe how Ben was feeling in the story.	Y1 (2) 10	New punctuation mark introduced: the dash.	Y1 (2) 2	Use of letter and picture cues to predict and check meanings of unfamiliar words, and to make sense of what the children read.	Y1 (2) 2	Children write about what they would like to do when they grow up.
The new baby	Story with familiar language	To read on sight 30 more high-frequency words to aid reading.	Y1 (2) 6	To use awareness of grammar of a sentence to decipher new and unfamiliar words.	Y1 (2) 2	Compare/contrast the styles of a 'fiction' and 'non-fiction' book. Take note of type of illustrations, layout, presentation of information and narrative structure.	Y1 (2) 17	Write a description of Poppa.
Baby Bear goes fishing	Story with elements of fantasy	Regular endings to present tense words: -ing; going; fishing; coming.	Y1 (2) 7	To self-correct by asking child to re-read to make the sentence make sense.	Y1 (2) 2	To re-read the story and look at significant incidents in the story. Contrast with *Father Bear goes fishing*	Y1 (3) 5	Write captions for a wall story or book about bear/fish facts that the children know.
Hermit Crab	Story with predictable structure	Look at initial consonant clusters related to the story, for example 'cr' – crab, creep, crash.	Y1 (2) 3	Draw attention to why some words are written in italics.	Y1 (2) 1	To be aware that the story is a combination of narrated prose and rhyme. Learn the simple rhyme and re-read it from the text.	Y1 (2) 11	Make a book about homes for animals.
Sally and the sparrows	Story with predictable structure	Look at words with the long 'ee' sounds. Read parts of the story to hear the sound.	Y1 (3) 1	To expect reading to make sense and check if it does not through a variety of cues.	Y1 (3) 1	Re-tell the story, including the sequence of events and highlighting significant events, for example, what Sally's problem was and how she solved it.	Y1 (3) 5	Write a recount of their own experiences when they wake up at the weekend.
Choosing a puppy	Story with predictable structure	Make a new word list of words ending with 'y', for example 'Andy' and 'puppy'.	Y1 (3) 8	Aware of capital letters as cues to distinguish characters' names.	Y1 (2) 7	To identify and use established narrative conventions to re-tell the story from the dog's perspective.	Y1 (3) 6	Write a simple advert using one adjective. Discuss words that describe puppies.
Football at the park.	Story with predictable structure	Look at common spelling pattern, for example all/ball.	Y1 (3) 5	To be aware of the speech marks and to read 'like talking'.	Y1 (3) 3	To use a wide range of cues to work out, predict and check what has been read to ensure that the text makes sense.	Y1 (3) 2	Write a 'happy-sad' book.

YELLOW LEVEL (Set 3)

Title	Genre	Word level work	NLS	Sentence level work	NLS	Text level work	NLS	Writing extension	NLS
Seagull is clever	Story with predictable language	To recognise words by common spelling patterns, for example, looking at compound words such as 'shellfish' and 'seagull'.	Y1 (3) 5	If a word is difficult, give children three choices to check against the word and ask how they know that was right.	Y1 (3) 4	Use the book as an information text. Ask simple questions and use text to find answers.	Y1 (3) 19	Ask children to write labels to go with a picture of a bird.	Y1 (3) 19
Little Bulldozer	Story with elements of fantasy	Learn spellings with past and present tense endings, for example 'help', 'helping', 'helped', 'helps'.	Y1 (3) 6	To expect reading to make sense and check if it does not by matching the appearance of characters in the illustrations with what they are saying.	Y1 (3) 1	Compare and contrast stories on the theme of the contributions small characters can make. Look at the other animated story characters.	Y1 (3) 8	Add another page to the end of the story where Little Bulldozer helps again.	Y1 (3) 8
Sally's red bucket	Story with predictable language	To spell irregular words, for example 'come', 'came'.	Y1 (3) 7	Use awareness of grammar to decipher new or unfamiliar words for example sounding the 's' in 'Sally's.	Y1 (3) 2	Re-tell the main events of the story and look at significant incidents that happened to Sally and her Mum, using prediction skills.	Y1 (3) 5	Use the illustration on p14 and write about what happened when Mum and Sally went into the water.	Y1 (3) 5
A friend for little white rabbit	Story with patterned language	For children to hear words that begin the same way, for example words beginning with 'pl'.	Y1 (2) 3	To read the text with pace and expression with awareness of grammar, for example raising the voice for questions.	Y1 (3) 3	To extend the story about the friendship of the two rabbits.	Y1 (3) 14	Write a personal response to a part of the story.	Y1 (3) 14
Fire! Fire!	Story with predictable structure	Extend vocabulary by collecting new words about the text subject, for example 'helicopter', 'rescue'.	Y1 (3) 8	Reading the speech bubbles with expression.	Y1 (3) 3	Look at speech bubbles and compare them with other conventions used for direct speech.	Y1 (3) 3	Re-write page 4 and page 5 as 'straight text' without speech bubbles.	Y1 (3) 3
A Lucky Day for Little Dinosaur	Story with predictable structure	To look at irregular verbs 'go' and 'come'.	Y1 (3) 7	To encourage the child to build on the excitement of story by using punctuation cues, for example, bold and italic writing and exclamation marks.	Y1 (3) 3	For children to identify the part of the story they liked and why.	Y1 (3) 3	Write about dinosaur's breakfast.	Y1 (3) 4
Tiny and the big wave	Story with predictable language	Look at the common spelling patterns of words that end with 'y'.	Y1 (3) 5	Use word order to predict finding known and unknown words in sentence.	Y1 (3) 4	Look at the circular structure of story. Highlight beginning and end at signpost and the significant events in the middle.	Y1 (3) 5	Write a poem about waves using one adjective.	Y1 (3) 5
Snowy gets a wash.	Story with predictable structure	To read on sight the high-frequency word specific to the child's ability	Y1 (3) 2	To expect the reading to make sense and check if it does not.	Y1 (3) 1	To direct children to use a range of phonological, contextual, grammatical and graphic cues to help in making sense of what they are reading.	Y1 (3) 2	Write about the things Nick liked to do.	Y1 (3) 2

YELLOW LEVEL (Non-fiction)

Title	Genre	Word level work	NLS	Sentence level work	NLS	Text level work	NLS	Writing extension
My Dad	Observation recounts	Use the initial and medial letter sounds to make sense of a word, for example <u>w</u>ater and w<u>a</u>ves.	Y1 (2) 1	Notice that 'Dad' and 'Mum' start with a capital letter.	Y1 (2) 4	Study Dad and the girl. Compare size of clothes, feet, hands and so on. Look at the way they are dressed.	Y1 (3) 7	Make a 'helping' book.
Our Mum	Observation recounts	Find a word and use initial, medial or final letter sounds to work out word, for example 'library' – 'l', 'b', 'y'.	Y1 (2) 1	If a word is difficult, encourage the child to look at part of the word, re-read the sentence and think about where it would go.	Y1 (2) 3	To compare the family in story to the family in *My Dad*	Y1 (2) 8	Make a card for Mum.
My Little Sister	Observation recounts	To look at common spelling patterns by making word strings using b-g.	Y1 (1) 4	Offer choices of phrase for children to check against a difficult phrase to see if they look right.	Y1 (3) 4	Compare and contrast the language and content with *My Big Brother*. Discuss preferences.	Y1 (3) 10	Use the information in the book to make a character study of the little sister.
My Big Brother	Observation recounts	Learn spellings with 'ed' and 'ing' endings, for example use 'like' and 'bike'.	Y1 (3) 6	To see the changes between 'I', 'We', and 'He' at the beginning of sentences.	Y1 (2) 7	Investigate to see if there is a narrative structure and sequence in the story.	Y1 (3) 5	Use the information from the text to write about big brother.
Our Baby	Observation recounts	To segment words into phonemes for reading	Y1 (3) 1	Look at a sentence as a whole for cues to decipher unfamiliar words.	Y1 (3) 2	To look at the title page and cover to predict content. To become aware of the use of photographs to expand on the information given by the text.	Y1 (3) 7	Use the illustration on p5 to write speech bubbles for the characters.
My Gran and Grandad.	Observation recounts	Look at the different names the children call their grandparents.	Y1 (3) 8	Show how the names of the children's grandparents start with a capital letter.	Y1 (3) 5	Look at the common themes in the 'family' series. Talk about the children's families.	Y1 (3) 10	Draw or paint pictures of their grandparents and write a caption.